D1596822

1. The Unquiet Heart

THE UNQUIET HEART

Reflections on Love and Sexuality

Jordan Aumann, O.P.
Dr. Conrad Baars

THE UNQUIET HEART

Reflections on Love and Sexuality

**
*

You have made us for yourself, O Lord,
and our hearts are restless until they rest in you.
(St. Augustine)

ALBA · HOUSE   NEW · YORK

SOCIETY OF ST. PAUL, 2187 VICTORY BLVD., STATEN ISLAND, NEW YORK 10314

Library of Congress Cataloging-in-Publication Data

Aumann, Jordan.
        The unquiet heart : reflections on love and sexuality /
    Jordan Aumann, Conrad Baars.
            p.   cm.
        Includes bibliographical references.
        Contents: Theology of love and sexuality / Jordan Aumann —
    Psychology of love and sexuality / Conrad W. Baars.
        ISBN 0-8189-0619-7
        1. Sex — Religious aspects — Catholic Church.
    2. Sex (Psychology)   3. Catholic Church — Doctrines.
    I. Baars, Conrad.   II. Title.
    BX1795.S48A85   1991   91-27910
    241'.66 — dc20   CIP

Censor Ordinis:
Reverend Dennis R. Zusy, OP

Imprimi Potest:
Most Reverend Donald J. Goergen, OP
Prior Provincial

Nihil Obstat:
Reverend Patrick J. Boyle, SJ
Censor Deputatus

Imprimatur:
Very Reverend John R. Gorman, D.D.
Vicar General, Archdiocese of Chicago
July 11, 1991

The Nihil Obstat and Imprimatur are official declarations that a book or
pamphlet is free of doctrinal or moral error. No implication is contained
therein that those who have granted the Nihil Obstat and Imprimatur agree
with the content, opinions or statements expressed.

Designed, printed and bound in the United States of
America by the Fathers and Brothers of the
Society of St. Paul, 2187 Victory Boulevard,
Staten Island, New York 10314, as part of their
communications apostolate.

PRINTING INFORMATION:

Current Printing - first digit   1   2   3   4   5   6   7   8   9   10   11   12

Year of Current Printing - first year shown

1991   1992   1993   1994   1995   1996   1997   1998

PREFACE

This book is addressed to all the faithful of Christ (*Christi-fideles*): married and unmarried laity, seminarians and priests, members of institutes of the consecrated life and secular institutes. Each and every person in these various states of life is called upon to strive for Christian maturity and for the perfection of charity. That doctrine was officially promulgated by the Second Vatican Council (cf. *Lumen Gentium*, no. 40). No longer, therefore, can anyone deny that all the faithful without exception are called to strive for Christian perfection. Neither can anyone propose that there are two paths to Christian holiness, one ordinary and the other extraordinary; rather, the mystical life is nothing more than the full flowering of the life of grace and charity.

We have deliberately linked together the two phrases: Christian maturity and the perfection of charity. This indicates that one normally needs an integrated human personality in order to arrive at the perfection of the Christian life. Moreover, we thereby recognize that both the psychologist and the theologian have something to say about maturity and Christian perfection.

Alba House has previously published two works co-authored by Conrad W. Baars, M.D. and Anna A. Terruwe, M.D., of Nijmegen, Holland. The first was published in 1976 under the title *Healing the Unaffirmed*; the second was published in 1981 and is entitled *Psychic Wholeness and Healing*.

Both Dr. Baars and Dr. Terruwe have made a significant contribution to psychiatry by distinguishing between the classical repressive neurosis described by Freud and the deprivation neurosis, which requires an essentially distinct type of therapy. Drawing upon their many years of psychiatric practice and their study of the philosophy and theology of St. Thomas Aquinas, they have formulated a therapy based on the Thomistic teaching that the human emotions are directed by nature to be guided by the rational powers of intellect and will.

This principle obviously is of great importance in any study of human love and sexuality, and we do not hesitate to refer to it frequently throughout this book. And if we need any defense for going back to the teaching of Aquinas, we find it in a statement made by Professor P.J. Calon of the University of Nijmegen: "Dr. Terruwe is fully justified in basing her work on Aquinas' teachings about the emotional life of man, as until now it has remained unsurpassed in excellence by any modern hypothesis."

Jordan Aumann, O.P.

ACKNOWLEDGMENTS

Grateful acknowledgment is made to the following publishers for quotations used in this book:

Collins Liturgical Publications, London: *The Code of Canon Law*, 1983.

Crossroad, New York: *Spiritual Passages* by Benedict Groeschel, 1983.

Crowell-Collier, New York: *The Image of Love* by Clemens Benda, 1961.

Devin-Adair, New York: *Walls Are Crumbling* by J. Oesterreicher, 1952.

Dominican Publications, Dublin: *Vatican Council II: Conciliar and Post Conciliar Documents*, ed. A. Flannery, 1977; *Vatican Council II: More Postconciliar Documents*, ed. A. Flannery, 1982.

Franciscan Herald Press, Chicago, Illinois: *About Love*, by Josef Pieper, 1974; *I Believe in Love* by F. Jamart, 1974.

Harcourt, Brace & World, Inc., New York: *The Four Loves* by C.S. Lewis, 1960.

Helicon Press, New York: *Living Today for God* by Roger Schutz, 1962.

B. Herder, St. Louis, Missouri: *Spirituality of Love* by C.V. Heris, 1965; *Spirituality of Archbishop Martinez* by J.G. Trevino, 1966; now distributed by TAN Books, Rockford, Illinois.

McGraw-Hill Book Company, New York: *Summa Theologiae* by St. Thomas Aquinas, Vol. 19 (1967); Vol. 5 (1967); Vol. 34 (1975); Vol. 43 (1967); Vol. 44 (1971); Vol. 47 (1973).

The Newman Press, Westminster, Maryland: *The Complete Works of St. John of the Cross,* tr. by E. Allison Peers, 1953; *The Law of Christ* by Bernard Häring, 1961.

W. W. Norton & Co., New York: *Love and Will* by Rollo May, 1969; *The Complete Psychological Works of Sigmund Freud,* ed. J. Strachey, 1962.

Notre Dame University Press, Notre Dame, Indiana: *The Four Cardinal Virtues* by Josef Pieper, 1966.

Our Sunday Visitor, Huntington, Indiana: *Celibate Love* by Paul Conner, 1979.

Pastoral Renewal, 840 Airport Blvd., P.O. Box 8617, Ann Arbor, Michigan: "Problems in the Development of Masculine and Feminine Character," by Steve Clark, November, 1980.

Paulist Press, Glen Rock, New Jersey: *The Church and Sex* by R.F. Trevett, 1959.

The Rockford Institute, Rockford, Illinois: *The Religion and Society Report,* May, 1990.

Rockliff Publishing Corp., London: *Essay on Human Love* by Jean Guitton.

St. Anthony Guild Press, Paterson, New Jersey: *The New American Bible,* 1970.

St. Meinrad Publications, St. Meinrad, Indiana: *The Abode of Love* by A.A. Terruwe, 1970.

Sheed & Ward, London: *Married in Friendship* by Paul Conner, 1987. Sheed & Ward, New York: *A Companion to the Summa* by Walter Farrell, 1945.

CONTENTS

Part Two:
PSYCHOLOGY OF LOVE AND SEXUALITY
Dr. Conrad Baars

THEOLOGY OF LOVE AND SEXUALITY

Jordan Aumann, O.P., S.T.D.

1. Human Love
2. The Love that is Charity
3. Marital Love
4. Celibate Love

1

HUMAN LOVE

We learn from Sacred Scripture and from theology that the very essence and core of the Christian life and holiness consist in love. Christ himself answered a question on this matter by stating the twofold precept of charity: "You shall love the Lord your God with your whole heart, with your whole soul, and with all your mind. This is the greatest and first commandment. The second is like it: You shall love your neighbor as yourself" (Mt 22:37-38).

At the same time we learn from observation and experience, especially in contemporary society, with its preoccupation with sensate gratification, that we are engulfed in a wave of the unrestrained enjoyment of everything and anything that caters to selfish pleasure. In spite of so much talk about social justice, community, and aid to persons in need, it is appalling to see the large number of persons whose interests and activities seldom rise above the level of the senses. The words of Juvenal could be applied to many of them: "they are worn out but not satiated." Of course, there have always been people whose primary pursuit is sensual pleasure; the difference today is that much of what was

traditionally forbidden as immoral or harmful to the individual
or society, has now been legalized.

The present situation is not one that developed within the
last few years or even the last few decades. It has its roots in the
revolt against Victorian morality and customs after the First
World War. One of the champions against that Victorian
puritanism and repression was Sigmund Freud, who taught that
the libido is the most natural and strongest instinctual drive in
the human being. Unfortunately, in his efforts to liberate sexuality, he practically annihilated man's free will and declared a state
of war between man's superego and his instinctual drives. As a
result, it seems, as Jean Guitton puts it, "as if nature had both
desired to summon man to love and, at the same time, allowed
him to be prevented from loving" (*Essay on Human Love,* p. 3).

This does not mean, however, that we can point to Freud as
a champion of exaggerated sexual freedom or that he would
approve of the effects of the sexual revolution in contemporary
society. On the contrary, he branded unrestrained sensate
gratification as harmful and destructive; he was intelligent
enough to see the importance of the control and proper channel-
ing of one's sexual energies. Thus, when speaking of the
tendency to "debasement in the sphere of love," he said:

> It can easily be shown that the psychical value of erotic needs
> is reduced as their satisfaction becomes easy. An obstacle is
> required in order to heighten libido; and where natural resist-
> ances to satisfaction have not been sufficient, men have at all
> times erected conventional ones so as to be able to enjoy love.
> This is true of both individuals and nations. In times in which
> there were no difficulties standing in the way of sexual
> satisfaction, such as perhaps during the decline of the ancient
> civilizations, love became worthless and life empty, and
> strong reaction-formations were required to restore indis-
> pensable affective values. . . .

The ascetic current in Christianity created psychical values for love which pagan antiquity was never able to confer on it (*The Complete Psychological Works of Sigmund Freud,* ed. J. Strachey, pp. 187-188).

In spite of the foregoing statement, the name of Freud has been used time and time again to justify the abandonment of all sexual restraints. We need but recall the widespread popularity of the Kinsey reports, which used clinical studies and statistics to demonstrate the universality of both normal and deviate sexual activity. More recently, the Masters-Johnson experiments concentrated on the mechanics and techniques of sexual activity. As a result, in the minds of many persons sexuality was restricted to genital activity, and in time love was equated with sex. In his book, *About Love,* Josef Pieper refers to the "perversion" of "making isolated sexuality into an 'absolute,' " and he places much of the blame on commercial motives and the techniques of advertising (p. 105).

Perhaps by this time a large number of persons have become disillusioned by the results of the sexual revolution and have begun to think that there must be other expressions of love that have nothing to do with physical sexuality. This, at least, is the opinion of Dr. Rollo May:

> The old myths and symbols by which we oriented ourselves are gone, anxiety is rampant; we cling to each other and try to persuade ourselves that what we feel is love; we do not will because we are afraid that if we choose one thing or one person, we'll lose the other, and we are too insecure to take that chance. . . . The individual is forced to turn inward; he becomes obsessed with the new form of the problem of identity, namely, Even-if-I-know-who-I-am, I-have-no-significance. I am unable to influence others. The next step is apathy. And the step following that is violence. For no human

being can stand the perpetually numbing experience of his
own powerlessness. . . .

The sexual form of love — lowest common denominator on
the ladder of salvation — understandably became our preoccupation; for sex, as rooted in man's inescapable biology,
seems always dependable to give at least a facsimile of love.
But sex, too, has become Western man's test and burden
more than his salvation. . . . . Most people seem to be aware on
some scarcely articulated level that the frantic quality with
which we pursue technique as our way to salvation is in direct
proportion to the degree to which we have lost sight of the
salvation we are seeking. It is an old and ironic habit of human
beings to run faster when we have lost our way; and we grasp
more fiercely statistics and technical aids in sex when we have
lost the values and meaning of love. . . .

There is obviously one thing left to revolt against, and that is
sex itself. The frontier, the establishing of identity, the valida-
tion of the self can be, and not infrequently does become for
some people, a revolt against sexuality entirely. I am certainly
not advocating this. What I wish to indicate is that the very
revolt against sex . . . is rumbling at the gates of our cities or, if
not rumbling, at least hovering. The sexual revolution comes
finally back on itself, not with a bang but a whimper (*Love and
Will*, pp. 13-15; 60-61).

It should be evident, as Dr. Clemens Benda has pointed
out, that "if love is merely a transient physiological need, like
hunger, that must be satisfied to rid oneself of a disturbing force,
the years of man's life that are dominated by sexuality are
wasted. The fire of Eros burns out without having served to
mold a new personality. . . . The present-day concept of man,
which sets his biological and material needs at the top of the

scale as most urgent, while all psychological and spiritual forces are considered superimposed, 'inhibiting' factors, considers man essentially an animal" (*The Image of Love*, pp. 15; 22-24). Yet, we would be guilty of a flight from reality if we were to deny that there always has been and always will be a tension or struggle between the demands of the flesh and our spiritual powers. Long before Christian writers like St. Paul described this internal warfare, the Greek philosopher Plato compared this conflict to a team of horses pulling in opposite directions. St. Augustine also comes to mind as a man who knew from experience what a long and arduous struggle it is to gain control of the sexual urge.

Unfortunately, the mere recognition of the conflict between the flesh and the spirit was interpreted by some as an irreconcilable opposition between the two, with the result that Christians were prompted to equate sexuality with sin. They were thus placed in an either-or situation and sometimes used excessively harsh ascetical practices in order to repress the so-called "concupiscible" love as well as the sex instinct. In its own way, this attitude was as erroneous and harmful as the contemporary tendency to identify love with sexuality. Many Christians have been placed in the difficult position of having to choose between the flesh and the spirit. This in spite of the fact that they should know both from experience and from the teaching of Christ that the world of the flesh and sexuality does not necessarily have to be pitted against the world of the spirit. Jean Guitton tried to set the balance right in his book, *Essay on Human Love*:

> Perhaps it has not been sufficiently noted that there is in Christianity another current of thought which has not had the good fortune to find interpreters as popular as St. Paul. . . . When one deals with love from the point of view of the moralist, one can hardly avoid the idea of safeguarding morality. From this angle it is well to insist on the conflicts; but that

has the effect of infecting words with a contrary, adverse significance. Thus, the word *flesh* will not readily recover from the sombre sense given it by St. Paul. St. John, however, did not follow St. Paul in this respect; for him, since the Word made his abode in it, the flesh was a neutral, not a damnable element (p. 11).

After many decades of treating each other as opponents, theologians, psychologists and psychiatrists have finally admitted that they have much to offer to each other. Today a priest would be foolhardy to engage in counselling or spiritual direction without first acquainting himself with the basics of normal and abnormal psychology. On the other hand, no psychologist or psychiatrist can ignore the tremendous influence of religious belief and practice on the lives of most people. Consequently, both priests and psychiatrists now realize the need to complement each other and at times to refer patients to one another. They must, in a word, respect one another's area of specialization. The priest deals with spiritual and moral values; the psychiatrist and the psychologist deal with human functions on the natural level. The supernatural order lies outside the competence of the psychiatrist, unless, of course, he is also somewhat of an expert in theology. Normally, however, the supernatural is for the psychiatrist and psychologist "factor x" or the unknown factor.

We are not, of course, setting up a complete dichotomy between science and religion; we are far beyond that attitude of the materialists of the nineteenth century. There can be a very fruitful interchange between theologians and scientists. This was very clearly spelled out in an article published in *The Religion & Society Report* of January, 1990. The article deals with a lecture given by Professor Jerome Lejeune of Paris, discoverer of the Downs Syndrome, at the Pope John Paul II Institute in Washington, D.C., and it deserves to be quoted here:

Lejeune asserts as a scientific truth a claim long familiar to theologians and philosophers: "In his quest for the truth, the biologist comes upon a twofold evidence at the two extremes of the development of a human being. This evidence is clear: spirit animates matter. . . ." Lejeune goes on to argue that the nature of human reproduction and our knowledge of the genetic code morally obliges us to recognize that the developing embryo is a human life from conception and requires that we do all that is in our power to respect it and to protect it.

It is rather a truism in scientific circles that science tells us the way things are, but does not tell us how they ought to be, what they ought to do, how we ought to act. Frequently this important distinction is ignorantly or deliberately overlooked, as when, for example, sociological observations of how certain people behave, or were alleged to behave, while *Coming of Age in Samoa* (Margaret Mead) are put forward as prescriptions of how we ought to behave in the United States today. On the whole, however, most scientists do not claim that our moral duties can be deduced from their experimental data.

Professor Lejeune, *par contre*, contends that what we are learning about the nature of things, or rather, to be more specific, about the nature of human beings, does tell us how we ought to act towards others and, of course, towards ourselves. Lejeune's theory is an example of natural law ethics, but it differs from the traditional natural law ethics of Thomas Aquinas and those who follow him in being based not on *general principles and presuppositions* about the "nature" and the "natural end" of human beings and activities, but on some *very detailed and specific scientific data.* . . . An understanding of the *nature* of things (and of people), which science can help us to attain, may give us moral insights concerning what we ought to do in specific cases, provided that a prior conviction about fundamental principles exists and is generally accepted. . . . The existence of a prior conviction is what permits scientists such as Lejeune to argue from scientific facts to moral duties, as in the following example: "When technology gives us control over the very young human being, over the embryo which can be formed in a quasi-alchemical phial, and even brought back from a frozen state, this natural morality teaches us that young as he might be, as fragile as he might be, the human embryo is a member of our species and by that fact ought to be protected from all exploitation. . . . He is quite precisely our neighbor, our likeness, the flesh of our flesh.

It follows, therefore, that from the very nature of our topic — love and sexuality in the Christian life — we should discuss it from both a psychological and a theological perspective. A purely theological, or indeed moralistic, approach could easily lead us into that "angelism" that was characteristic of the puritanical Victorian age and also of a good deal of traditional books and treatises on the spiritual life of Christians. On the other hand, a purely psychological approach would almost certainly run the risk of identifying love and sexuality with purely sensate gratification. We want to avoid both of those extremes by integrating the principles of psychology with the teaching of theology.

Our Wounded Nature

Our task is to investigate the role of sex and love in the life of a human being in order to know how to establish the proper balance and integration between these two vital forces in the Christian life. The goal of every Christian, as of every human being, should be to attain the maturity of an integrated person. Only then is it possible to live the fullness of the Christian life. But this in turn requires the proper correlation between love and sexuality, avoiding the extremes of sex without love and love without feeling.

Moreover, a correct understanding of love and sexuality requires a correct understanding of the nature of the human being, created by God in the image of God and called to a perfection and happiness that infinitely exceed the powers of pure nature. As the poet Wordsworth put it, "Trailing clouds of glory, we come from God, who is our home."

But unfortunately, as we learn from Sacred Scripture, at the very beginning of human history there was a first, an original sin (cf. Gn 3:1-24). Without a firm belief in this doctrine of the faith, the problem of love and sexuality would be insoluble. Indeed, had there been no original sin, there would have been no need of redemption and God would not have promised to send a Messiah. Thus, as Matthias Scheeben says, both Adam and Christ are universal men; we are born in Adam and reborn in Christ. But the mysteries of original sin and redemption are known to us only through divine revelation, and then only in part (*Mysteries of Christianity*, p. 13).

What we do know, however, is that the human race has been wounded or hurt. For example, we read in the Book of Genesis that before the sin, "the man and his wife were both naked, yet they felt no shame" (Gn 2:25). But after their sin, "the eyes of both of them were opened, and they realized that they were naked; so they sewed fig leaves together and made loincloths for themselves" (Gn 3:7). And note that their sense of shame is not described as something that was induced in them from without, but as something natural and deeply rooted in human nature. The sense of shame is, in fact, a fundamental proof of our freedom of choice and a justification for feelings of guilt when our choice is morally wrong.

Although composed of body and soul, the human being lives and functions as a unit, a person. Hence the instinctive need to integrate these two elements and hence also the harmful effects of judging them to be incompatible or even mutually antagonistic. But the effects of original sin and also the traces of our own personal sins make it that much more difficult to achieve the harmony of an integrated personality and to reach the goal for which God created us. Difficult, but not impossible, because we have been redeemed through the passion and death of Christ, through the merits of which we can receive the grace that elevates us to the status of children of God. Then, as God's children, if we cooperate with grace, we can achieve the fullness of Christian maturity and perfection. And the pathway to that perfection and maturity is love.

Love in General

It is axiomatic in psychology that our knowledge of external reality first comes to us through the external senses, which are the points of contact with that reality. This sense knowledge, in turn, normally stimulates a reaction in our feelings or emotions so that we are attracted to that which pleases us or we experience an aversion for that which displeases us or is judged to be offensive or harmful. If it is a question of being attracted to something pleasing to us, we experience a certain complacency or attraction to the object of our affection. The intensity of the feeling will vary, depending on the object itself, the degree of sensate stimulation, or the habits, mood, temperament or tastes of the individual. Nevertheless, every person is naturally drawn to that which pleases or is seen as a good, and this attraction is given the name of love. Hence, the philosopher will speak of one's love for a dish of ice cream or a beautiful red rose as readily as he will speak of one's love for another person.

In his *Summa Theologiae* St. Thomas Aquinas puts it this way: "Natural things desire what is in conformity with their nature. . . . In every appetite or desire, love is the principle of the movement that tends towards that which is loved. In the natural appetite the principle of the movement is the connaturality that exists between the one who desires and the end to which he tends. We may call it a *natural love*. . . . Natural love is not restricted to the vegetative powers of the soul; it is found in all the faculties of the soul, in all parts of the body, and indeed in all created things" (I-II, q. 26).

Although the knowledge and love of external material things are experiences of everyday life, we also have an awareness of self and of the needs of our human organism as well as a desire to satisfy those needs. This is something innate and instinctual and it constitutes the first law of nature, that of self-preservation. At first it is directed to the well-being of the individual (the sensed need for nutrition, for example); later it is directed to the well-being of the species (the awakening of the sex instinct). Both the instinctual desire for food and sex and the sensate knowledge and love of external material things will be experienced by animals as well as by human beings. But as a composite of body and soul, flesh and spirit, the human person is capable of sublimating these experiences and enjoying them in a way that an animal could never do. For that reason the instinctual needs and sensate affections of a human being can never be fully explained or appreciated by equating them with those of the animal world. Nevertheless, it is possible that a person may ignore the dictates of reason and operate exclusively on a sensate or emotional level, as happens when an individual concentrates solely on a sensate gratification or operates on an exclusively emotional level.

Purely physical gratifications may satisfy for a time, but by their very nature they are short-lived. Indeed, they have a definite threshold beyond which pleasure becomes pain and revelry becomes exhaustion. The human spirit seeks something more than a particular sensate satisfaction; it has a thirst for the transcendent. Therefore, sensate pleasure can never slake its thirst for the absolute, for eternal happiness. For this reason the theologians maintain that the human being has a natural desire for God; so much so that Voltaire stated that if there were no God, man would create one.

One should not conclude from the foregoing, however, that it is necessary to disdain and reject all created goods and the satisfactions they offer. That would be going against nature and would therefore be contrary to biblical teaching: "God looked at everything he had made, and he found it very good" (Gn 1:31). The material goods of this world are true goods and normally the path that leads to God begins with creatures. If loved and used rightly, there is no danger that these created goods and sensate gratifications will ever become obstacles to one's love of God and of neighbor. They may in fact become signs and symbols of love, as are the bread and wine in the Eucharist or the marital embrace of husband and wife. As St. John of the Cross stated:

> Although it is true that the soul cannot help hearing and seeing and smelling and tasting and touching, this is of no greater import, nor, if the soul denies and rejects the object, is it hindered more than if it saw it not, heard it not, etc. . . . We are not treating here of the lack of things, since this implies no detachment on the part of the soul if it has a desire for them; but we are treating of the detachment from them of the taste and desire, for it is this that leaves the soul free and void of them, although it may have them; for it is not the things of this world that occupy the soul or cause it harm, since they enter it not, but rather the will and desire for them, for it is these that dwell within it (*Ascent of Mount Carmel*, I, 3, 4, Peers translation).

Another point that needs to be discussed is the correct evaluation of self-love. According to the twofold precept of love given by Christ, we are to love God above all things and to love our neighbor. But what of love of self? What does this precept do to self-preservation as the first law of nature? If one had asked these questions of Christ, he might very well have answered that there is no need to tell a person to love himself, since this is a natural, innate love. Note that Christ told us to "love your neighbor *as yourself*" (Mt 22:38). In fact, love of self can be a problem because, as Joseph Pieper has pointed out, "since the first sin, man has been not only capable of loving himself more than he loves God his Creator but, contrary to his own nature, inclined to do so" (*The Four Cardinal Virtues*, p. 150). As a result, one needs to cultivate the virtue of temperance, which moderates the gratification of the sense appetites, and the virtue of justice, which respects the rights of others and prompts one to fulfill his or her duties to others. Consequently, these two virtues are of utmost importance in the moral formation of the young, in whom self-centered love tends to be a dominant force.

The ease with which human beings go to excess in love of self has prompted some spiritual writers to go to extremes in urging Christians to transcend self-love. We must remember that the created goods that we need for life and self-perfection (useful goods) or those that we need for the joy of living (pleasurable goods) are always desired and sought with a view to self. They are loved with a self-centered love, a love that begins with self, goes out to the object loved, and brings it back to self. It is a love that is fully in conformity with our human nature, and therefore morally good. It becomes morally wrong only when it goes contrary to the requirements and demands of the controlling virtues of temperance or justice.

The ancient Scholastic terminology, concupiscible love (*amor concupiscentiae*) and benevolent or friendship love (*amor amicitiae*), is not much used by contemporary theologians. In fact, the very word "concupiscible" may too easily be interpreted as something purely selfish, if not morally wrong. Nevertheless, St. Thomas Aquinas used those terms to make a very important distinction. When the movement of love is towards a *thing* that is desired, that love is called concupiscible love, because things are loved not for themselves but for the one who loves and desires them. Thus, we love food for ourselves and we love and desire an automobile for our own use. But when the movement of love terminates in a *person,* that is called friendship or benevolent love because we wish good to the person who is loved. St. Thomas then concludes that since we are *persons,* our rightly ordered love of self is in no sense reprehensible. "Our love for ourselves," he says, "is the model and root of friendship, because our friendship for others consists precisely in the fact that our attitude towards them is the same as towards ourselves" (cf. *Summa Theologiae,* I-II, 25, 2).

Does this mean, then, that all love of neighbor is at basis a self-centered love? Do we really love our friends for selfish reasons? This can and does occur when we love a person as a thing, simply an object of our own gratification or benefit, but in this case concupiscible, self-centered love has usurped the place of friendship love. In authentic friendship love a person's affection goes out to the beloved as a *person* for whom one wishes some good, and he works for it for the sake of his friend and not for himself (cf. *Summa Theologiae,* I-II, q. 28).

So much for the consideration of love in general. We turn now to a discussion of the various types of love that are experienced by the human being on the physical, emotional and volitional levels. And since we are concerned primarily with the integration of sexuality with love, we shall correlate these two elements whenever possible.

Physical Love

The human person lives and acts on three different levels: the physical, the emotional and the rational. Consequently, there is a natural appetite or love that is the stimulant for activity on each of these levels. Love on the purely physical level has been given a variety of names: natural appetite, instinct, body needs, sub-human love or simply physical love.

Unlike love at the higher levels, physical or instinctual love does not require previous knowledge for its stimulation, although the individual quickly becomes aware of the stirring of an instinct or the urges and demands of his or her bodily needs. Thus, the pangs of hunger or the sexual urge will make their demands felt according to the physiological laws that regulate those functions; and once they are satisfied, they will be at rest until the need or urge makes itself felt again. These are natural urges but they are also the most powerful physical forces of self-preservation in the human being. For that reason, says J. Pieper, "they exceed all other powers of mankind in their destructive violence once they degenerate into selfishness" (*The Four Cardinal Virtues*, p. 150).

Considered simply as organic functions, the bodily instincts are as restricted in their purpose as are the functions of other bodily organs. The reason for eating and drinking is to provide nutrition for the body; the purpose of the physical act of sex is the reproduction of the human species. There may well be other reasons for eating and for sex, depending on the motivation of the individual, but this does not change the natural purpose of these functions. And since both of these physical activities can be the source of intense sensate pleasure, it is not surprising that some individuals will use them primarily or exclusively for selfish gratification.

Physical love in the sexual context may be called *genital sexuality*; since it has to do with the desire for the physical act of sex. But as a human function it will always call into play the emotions, the intellect and the will. Dr. Clemens Benda has succeeded very well in describing the physical aspect of genital sexuality and then placing it in proper perspective:

In the animal kingdom the sex drive is not present throughout the year but appears in certain rhythms. During such periods the animal is subject to increased tension and irritability which affect its total behavior. The creature is driven until it finds a mate . . . and thus to find release. . . . Sexuality is an impersonal force under which the creatures have to discharge their roles. Animals do not *face* each other in sex but turn their heads away while submitting to its compulsion.

Man as a part of nature is subjected to sexuality, which he experiences as a drivenness foreign to the ego. The sexual instinct is not directed toward a specific person as object but toward gratification of itself. The other person acts as a means of satisfaction rather than an equal partner. Sexual aberrations clearly demonstrate this aspect. People feel driven by a power beyond their control and are acting out their needs, while the mutuality — so essential to a love experience — is missing.

If the principle of gratification is proclaimed the highest law governing sex relations, one may ask why it is that satisfaction is not found wherever physical gratification is provided. . . . Why does fulfillment not necessarily generate gratitude and love but often produces hostility and hate?

The answer to these questions lies in the fact that two human beings united in sexuality may discover that the gratification they have found has not satisfied *them* but a desire *in* them. They have been in bondage to an urge with which they no longer feel identified when their need is stilled. The very fact that the other can get hold of us, can possess us because we are temporarily prey to an emotion that overrides our full personality, generates germs of resentful hostility if one feels used for the sake of bodily satisfaction and not loved and needed as an individual (*The Image of Love*, pp. 14-16, *passim*).

Although the intensity of the sexual drive varies with individuals, the fact remains that the physical, sexual urge seeks its own release and satisfaction. Something else is needed to prevent individuals from becoming blind instruments of their genital sexuality, and this should be provided by reasonable control through the virtue of temperance (and specifically by the virtues of chastity and continence). If this be lacking, only the law or the fear of disease or sin will serve as inhibiting factors. As R.F. Trevett puts it: "The law forbids sexual sins. It attempts to do for man what instinct does for the brute beasts: to supply a norm by which we can lead our sex lives without grave harm to others and to ourselves" (*The Church and Sex*, p. 19).

But if the physical act of sex is performed with due regard for the persons involved, then the rational powers of the human being will come into play and elevate genital sexuality above the purely animal level. The aggressive aspect of genital sexuality will be reduced and the two persons will be able to give themselves to each other in an act of generous love. Thus, Dr. Benda continues:

> Facing each other, man and woman are no longer the prey of an impersonal force that throws them together; the sex act has become an act of mutual acceptance, an act of choice. Facing each other brings all sensual perceptions into action: seeing, hearing, smelling, touching. The individuals are not reduced to performing a genital act; the whole body is involved. The awareness of the other's total personality demands full commitment. It brings about an element of inhibition that prohibits the most intimate relatedness with any person not chosen. Sex thus becomes the most complete expression of an involvement between two human beings in which each has ceased to be a separate entity. The body is the last that can be given and forfeited when everything else has been surrendered (*op. cit.*, p. 19).

What, then, of the morality of genital sexuality? From what we have said, it should be recognized that the sex instinct and genital sexuality are good in themselves, as is true of all the other body needs and instincts. Therefore it is perfectly natural and lawful to satisfy them, but under the proper conditions. The use and enjoyment of genital sexuality are morally wrong in the following circumstances: *when the use and enjoyment of genital sexuality lead to excess* (every excess is a vice, and hence the need for marital chastity); *when sexual activity is contrary to the very purpose of genital sexuality* (masturbation, artificial contraception, the use of the pill, the practice of homosexuality); *the use and enjoyment of genital sexuality contrary to some positive law that forbids it* (divine positive law restricts the use and enjoyment of sex to husband and wife; positive ecclesiastical law requires celibacy of priests in the Latin rite and of persons in the consecrated life).

The Emotion of Love

When discussing the emotions, psychologists usually describe two steps in the emotional experience: first, there must be sensate knowledge of an object judged to be pleasant or unpleasant, useful or harmful, to the percipient; secondly, a psychosomatic reaction in the individual as a result of this evaluation. Involving as they do both sensate awareness and an organic reaction, the emotions are common to both human beings and animals. They are therefore morally neutral or indifferent when considered in themselves. In human beings, however, the emotional experience may relate to reason and will in three ways. First, an emotional outburst may *precede* any act of the will, as in the case of spontaneous anger or fright. Secondly, the activation of an emotion may *accompany* the act of the will, as when the emotion of love accompanies one's fond recollection of a loved one or a person advances to a confrontation with fear. Finally, the emotional response may *follow upon* or be stimulated by an act of the will, as when one deliberately works himself into a state of anger or courage. But it is only when intellect and will intervene sufficiently in relation to the emotional experience that there can be a question of personal responsibility, and hence of the morality of the emotional reaction.

The emotion of love falls within the category of the "pleasure emotions" (also called the concupiscible passions) as distinct from the "utility emotions" (known as the irascible passions). And since all the emotions are reactions to a perceived object evaluated in terms of self, emotional love is essentially a self-centered love. It can be called by various names — affection, need-love, sensate love, self-centered love — and it may be described as a feeling of complacency towards an object that is seen as good and pleasing to the percipient. The moralist may be tempted to brand all emotional love as "mere selfishness," no doubt because such expressions as "selfish," "self-centered" and "concupiscible" easily connote an excessive preoccupation with one's ego. But C.S. Lewis puts us on our guard against such an erroneous concept:

> We must be cautious about calling need-love "mere selfishness." *Mere* is always a dangerous word. No doubt need-love, like all our impulses, can be selfishly indulged. A tyrannous and gluttonous demand for affection can be a horrible thing. But in ordinary life no one calls a child selfish because it turns for comfort to its mother; nor an adult who turns to his fellow "for company." Those, whether children or adults, who do so least are not usually the most selfless. Where need-love is felt there may be reasons for denying or totally mortifying it; but not to feel it is in general the mark of the cold egoist. Since we do in reality need one another . . . then the failure of this need to appear as need-love in consciousness . . . is a bad spiritual symptom; just as lack of appetite is a bad medical symptom because men really do need food (*The Four Loves*, pp. 12-13, *passim*).

The truth of the matter is that the emotion of love is both natural and morally good when rightly used. Our love for others and even our love for God should involve our entire being, including the emotion of love. When persons experience human love, the entire person, body and soul, will be involved in the process. A purely spiritual love, without any resonance on the emotional level, would be incomplete and defective as a *human* experience. A psychological reason for this is that as body-soul composites we can establish contact with the loved and desired object only through our external and internal senses. And once the judgment has been made concerning the goodness and desirability of the perceived object, there will necessarily follow a reaction in the psychosomatic structure, however faint.

Of course, it could happen that the desire that springs from emotional love is so intense that it dominates one's actions to such an extent that self-control is impossible. Such would usually be the case of persons suffering from a neurosis; they are governed, not by reason, but by an emotion. In fact, any one of several emotions, for example, fear, hatred, anger, sadness, can tyrannize an individual who has lost control of his or her emotional life. But healthy and balanced individuals will live according to the principle stated by St. Thomas Aquinas, namely, that the appetites or emotions are intended by nature to be obedient to reason. This is in a special way the function of the virtue of prudence, which is also the virtue that marks maturity, since it determines what is the right thing to do under given circumstances.

When the object of love and desire is sexual gratification, it gives rise to what we may call "psychic sexuality." For sexuality, like love, is operative on three distinct levels: the physical (genital sexuality), the psychic (stimulation of the emotions of love and desire) and the volitional (genetic sexuality). Since some psychiatrists divide the human composite into body, psyche and soul, and since by the term "psyche" they are referring to the mind as the center of one's thought, feelings and behavior, it would seem to be permissible to use the term "psychic sexuality." Soloviev used the expression "pathetic sexuality," meaning the tender feeling of love for another, but in today's language the word "pathetic" usually refers to feelings of pity, sadness, regret or even contempt.

Psychic sexuality is stimulated when an individual feels a definite attraction to another person because of certain sensate qualities or physical attributes of that person; for example, physical beauty, a pleasant smile, or an outgoing manner. One experiences a strong desire to be physically near that person, to get to know that person. And if the attraction is mutual, a current of sympathy (in the French and Spanish meaning of the word) is established between them. As a result, they are prompted to seek out each other's company, to enjoy physical nearness and to prolong the encounter as much as possible. In the interim between their meetings, there will be the exchange of letters, telephone calls and gifts. Sooner or later their love will seek expression by means of physical contact — the holding of hands, the kiss, the embrace. Emotional love between two persons, whether of the same sex or the opposite sex, will normally seek expression on the physical level, but it does not necessarily gravitate toward genital sexuality. The one can exist without the other: the emotion of love without a sexual connotation or the mere physical gratification without any feeling of love.

However, as long as love remains on the emotional level of psychic sexuality, it will still be largely concentrated on self, on the delight one experiences in being in love and in being loved in return. At this stage lovers have reached the "moment of decision" because psychic sexuality can move in either of two directions: toward the gratification of self through genital sex or the cultivation of the generous love of friendship, which should characterize the married state. Their love needs wings in order to transcend self, and these wings are supplied by Eros.

Unfortunately, this is another word that has lost its original meaning. As used today, the word "erotic" signifies that which stimulates sexual desire or lust, but among the ancients it meant something quite different, as Dr. Rollo May has explained:

> Eros in our day is taken as a synonym for "eroticism" or sexual titillation. . . . One wonders whether everyone has forgotten the fact that Eros, according to no less an authority than St. Augustine, is the power which drives men toward God. . . .
>
> Sex can be defined . . . in physiological terms as consisting in the building up of bodily tensions and their release. Eros, in contrast, is the experiencing of the personal intentions and meaning of the act. . . . The end toward which sex points is gratification and relaxation, whereas Eros is a desiring, long-ing, a forever reaching out, seeking to expand. . . .
>
> Eros . . . takes wings from human imagination and is forever transcending all techniques, giving the laugh to all the "how to" books, by gaily swinging into orbit above our mechanical rules, making love rather than manipulating organs. . . .
>
> Eros seeks union with the other person in delight and passion, and the procreating of new dimensions of experience which broaden and deepen the being of both persons. . . . It is this urge for union with the partner that is the occasion of human tenderness. For Eros — not sex as such — is the source of tenderness. Eros is the longing to establish union, full rela-tionship. . . . We have been led astray . . . to think that the aim of the love act is the orgasm. The French have a saying which . . . carries more truth: "The aim of desire is not its satisfaction but its prolongation" (*Love and Will*, pp. 72-75, *passim*).

In a sense, emotional love and psychic sexuality are a bridge between physical love and volitional love, between genital sexuality and genetic sexuality. At the same time, as Dr. Rollo May has pointed out, there is a dialectic between genital sexuality and psychic sexuality (Eros). The physical gratification of sex causes the individual to turn inward, to be concerned with his or her sensate pleasure and, indeed, to become preoccupied with the techniques of sex. In psychic sexuality or Eros, as St. Thomas Aquinas taught, "the lover is carried out of himself in a certain sense, insofar as not being content with enjoying what is already in his possession, he desires to enjoy something outside himself" (*Summa Theologiae*, I-II, 28, 3).

But the "ecstasy" of psychic sexuality is fundamentally an emotional experience, and since all emotional activity begins and ends in the one who experiences the emotion, psychic sexuality does not of itself suffice for the perfection of human love. For this, one must advance to a higher type of love — friendship love — in which a person's love terminates entirely outside of self. This occurs, says St. Thomas Aquinas, when the lover desires some good thing for the friend and works for it for the sake of the friend (*loc. cit.*). This would seem to indicate that friendship-love is something quite different from emotional or psychic love, and so it is. Before treating of that, however, it may be helpful to discuss briefly the differences between man and woman as regards emotional love and psychic sexuality.

First of all, there is less physiological difference between man and woman than we have thought, but there is much more psychic difference than we have been willing to admit. However, as psychologists have discovered, there is enough similarity between male and female as to leave a "ghost image" of the opposite sex in each one. There are traces of the feminine in the male that are especially evident during childhood and adolescence; on the other hand, most women develop certain masculine traits after menopause. But men and women are meant to complement each other and not compete with each other. Ideally, this duality of psychic sexual differences should contribute greatly to the fostering of love between a man and a woman. The reason for this can be found in the very nature of emotional love.

The Lord commanded Moses to give a series of precepts to the whole Israelite community and among them was the command: "You shall love your neighbor as yourself." Accordingly, it would seem that love of self, the first law of nature, is the foundation or springboard for love of others. But the emotion of love, as we have seen, is stimulated by an attraction to some sensed pleasurable or useful good. There must therefore be some sort of rapport or likeness between the lover and the object of love. Persons or things that are different, strange or even threatening do not automatically arouse a feeling of love in us. This underlines the fact that all emotions begin with self and terminate in the self. It is always a question of how the known object affects *me*.

But the likeness or similarity that stimulates the emotion of love has two different aspects: actual likeness and potential likeness. When there is an actual likeness or rapport, the object sensed as good for self will be loved as a reflection of self. In that sense the lover is, as it were, loving himself in the other. But if it is a question, for example, of loving a person who possesses something that we lack, but desire as a fulfillment of ourselves, then that likeness is only potential. And the love that springs from this potential likeness is also a love that is based on love of self.

Does this mean that it is impossible for the emotion of love ever to be the generous, benevolent love of friendship? The answer would seem to be that *of itself* the emotion of love can never rise to the level of friendship love, although it may accompany that love. Emotions are psychosomatic reactions to an object known through the senses, but friendship love requires the intervention of the intellect and will, as we shall see later.

Returning for the moment to the psychological differences between men and women; we can all verify these differences by observation and experience in daily life. Dr. Baars discusses the psychic sexual differences in greater detail in Part Two of this book. But in this age of the demand for sexual equality, it may be helpful to treat briefly of the problem of achieving sexual identity in contemporary society.

In his excellent book, *Man and Woman in Christ*, Steve Clark has stated that the lack of a masculine identity is usually found in the "socially disruptive" man and in the "feminized" man. A man is considered socially disruptive when he asserts his masculinity in an uncontrolled or irresponsible way. "The popular masculine caricature of the impersonal, unexpressive, unemotional, rugged individual is not the ideal for the Christian man," says Clark. At the other extreme we have the "feminized" man who has been so dominated by women — usually his mother — that he has learned to behave and react in a feminine way. "The feminized male," says Clark, "can be normal as a male, with no tendencies to reject being male and no tendencies toward homosexuality, and yet he can have been so influenced by women or can have so identified himself with a world in which women dominate that many of his interests and traits are more womanly than manly. . . . He will identify Christian virtue with feminine characteristics." As correctives, Clark suggests that disruptive males should be trained to take on social responsibilities; feminized or effeminate males should be taught to be more aggressive. A good relationship between father and son will enable the son to identify with his father and model himself after him.

As regards the feminine identity, Clark lists three types of women for whom womanliness is a problem. "The first is the woman who is characterized by a great deal of personal insecurity and dependence. Like the feminized man, this type of woman has often been overlooked by Christians because her tendencies toward submissiveness, self-abasement, and a great desire to please others are equated by many with charity, humility, and a gentle and quiet spirit. . . . She normally experiences a great deal of unhappiness and personal dissatisfaction and has a strong tendency to seek help."

The second type of woman who has a particular problem in this area is the "masculinized" woman, a parallel to the feminized man. These women behave and react in ways that are appropriate to men. Clark says that these women sometimes become masculinized "out of a lack of confidence that they will be accepted as women"; at other times they become masculinized because they feel that "male roles and activities are more important and provide greater security than female roles and activities. . . . Finally, women sometimes seem to become masculinized by the experience of competing with men in situations that are predominantly male in composition or standards."

The third type of woman who has difficulty in achieving a feminine identity is the one who has been influenced by the feminist movement, which seeks equality with men. Often such a woman appears to have "a more than ordinary amount of inner anger (frustration, resentment, bitterness) and often an assertiveness that is appropriate for neither a Christian man nor a Christian woman" (All quotations are from a condensation of Clark's book in *Pastoral Renewal*, November, 1980).

For both men and women it should be apparent that they will achieve inner peace and fulfillment only when they have a sense of their own particular and distinct identity and have accepted it. To a great extent the problems described by Steve Clark are the harvest we reap after the sexual revolution. Add to that, if you will, the rejection of moral values, the uncontrolled enjoyment of sensate pleasures, and the rampant secularism, and you have the recipe for the frustration, anxiety, and even violence that plague our society.

Volitional Love

In speaking of physical love and emotional love, we stated that both of those loves are essentially self-centered, "need" loves. They go out to the object loved because of some utilitarian or pleasurable aspect that will bring sensate satisfaction to the lover. Such is the nature of those two types of love; they are like two hands that reach out and bring the loved object back to self.

When, however, we rise to the level of the spiritual faculties of intellect and will, we discover the possibility (though not necessarily the guaranty) of a different kind of love that is proper to human beings. We call it volitional love because it involves the operation of the will (*voluntas* in Latin), whose specific activity is to love the good. The ancient Greeks called this love *philia*; Cicero described it as friendship-love; the theologians speak of it as benevolent love. Whatever the name that is used, volitional love is a generous "gift" love rather than a personal "need" love, although it will also contain some elements of love of self. That is not surprising if we keep in mind that the first law of nature is self-preservation and that even Sacred Scripture commands us to love others as we love ourselves. St. Thomas Aquinas provides us with a helpful distinction between self-centered need love and benevolent gift love:

> According to Aristotle (*Ethics*, VIII, 4), not all love has the character of friendship, but only that love which goes with wishing well, namely, when we so love another as to will what is good for him. For if we do not will what is good to the things we love, but rather we will their good for ourselves, as when we are said to love wine, a horse, or the like, then that is

not love of friendship but love of desire [concupiscible love]. For it would be foolish to say that someone has friendship with wine or a horse (*Summa Theologiae*, II-II, q. 23, art. 1).

Volitional love makes it possible for the lover to go out to the other person not as a mere object or thing, not for what that other person has or can give, but as a *person*, loved for what he or she is as a person. In order to do this, however, the lover must necessarily sacrifice — or better, rise above — self-centered interest. As we have seen, both physical and emotional love ultimately have self as their goal; they want to receive something; but the highest expression of volitional love consists in giving, not receiving. Note, however, that we can give without loving, but we cannot love at this level without giving. And when this gift love is reciprocated, when there is a mutual gift-love between persons, this constitutes friendship. "There," says Jean Guitton, "lies the difference between love and passion; the latter is nothing but love without sacrifice and consequently without gift" (*Essay on Human Love*, p. 80).

C.S. Lewis has noted that friendship love is "the least *natural* of loves" because the first law of nature is love of self, while friendship requires that we love the "other." For that reason, those persons who have never risen above the level of physical or emotional love, who see all human relationships as utilitarian or sensate, can hardly understand the meaning of authentic friendship-love. Conversely, those persons who go to excess in their love and concern for animals — even to the extreme of defending animals' "rights" — are foolishly attempting to raise animals to the level of human friendship.

There is a question, however, of the relationship between emotional or erotic love and the love of friendship. We have already stated that the emotion of love seeks physical nearness to the person loved and that it is expressed by means of affectionate glances, a special tone of voice, caressing and embracing, etc.

Human love and a budding friendship normally originate on the level of sensate knowledge which in turn stimulates the emotion of love. But friendship-love is not a mere feeling or emotion; it requires that the individuals involved transcend the purely emotional need-love and establish an interpersonal, loving relationship. The following lengthy quotation from C.S. Lewis deserves a careful reading:

> Without Eros none of us would have been begotten, and without affection none of us would have been reared; but we can live and breed without friendship. The species, biologically considered, has no need of it. The pack or herd — the community — may even dislike and distrust it. Headmasters and headmistresses and heads of religious communities, colonels and ships' captains, can feel uneasy when close and strong friendships arise between little knots of their subjects. . . .
>
> Again, that outlook which values the collective above the individual necessarily disparages friendship; it is a relationship between men at their highest level of individuality. It withdraws men from collective "togetherness" as surely as solitude itself could do; and more dangerously, for it withdraws them by two's and three's. Some forms of democratic sentiment are naturally hostile to it because it is selective and an affair of the few. To say "these are my friends" implies "those are not. . . ."
>
> This imposes on me at the outset a very tiresome bit of demolition. It has actually become necessary in our time to rebut the theory that every firm and serious friendship is really homosexual. The dangerous word *really* is here important. To say that every friendship is consciously and explicitly homosexual would be too obviously false; the wiseacres take refuge in the less palpable charge that it is *really*

— unconsciously, cryptically, in some Pickwickian sense —
homosexual. And this, though it cannot be proved, can never
of course be refuted. The fact that no positive evidence of
homosexuality can be discovered in the behavior of two
friends does not disconcert the wiseacres at all: "That," they
say gravely, "is just what we should expect." The very lack of
evidence is thus treated as evidence; the absence of smoke
proves that the fire is very carefully hidden. Yes — if it exists
at all. But we must first prove its existence. Otherwise we are
arguing like a man who should say: "If there were an invisible
cat in that chair, the chair would look empty; but the chair
does look empty; therefore there is an invisible cat in it."

The rest of us know that though we can have erotic love and
friendship for the same person, yet in some ways nothing is
less like a friendship than a love-affair. Lovers are always
talking to one another about their love; friends hardly ever
about their friendship. Lovers are normally face to face,
absorbed in each other; friends, side by side, absorbed in
some common interest. Above all, Eros (while it lasts) is
necessarily between two only. But two, far from being the
necessary number for friendship, is not even the best. And the
reason for this is important.

In each of my friends there is something that only some other
friend can fully bring out. By myself I am not large enough to
call the whole man into activity. . . . Hence true friendship is
the least jealous of loves. Two friends delight to be joined by a
third, and three by a fourth, if only the newcomer is qualified
to become a real friend (*The Four Loves*, pp. 88-92, *passim*).

From what we have said it should be evident that there is a
vast difference between physical and emotional love and volitional love; it is the difference between personal need-love
and generous gift-love. Moreover, it should be evident that love
will be more authentically human to the extent that volitional,
generous love predominates over the lower types of love. "Man

is a being who grows, even psychically," says Dr. Anna Terruwe, "and it is precisely characteristic of this psychic growth that sensory experience becomes more and more assimilated into the spiritual. A child is still completely determined by sensory experience. In puberty reason begins to take over from feeling and emotion. But this process advances very gradually. Only with the passing of adolescence does a person arrive at that adult stage in which feeling and emotion are completely integrated into reason. Then only does a person become genuinely and fully a mature human person" (*The Abode of Love*, p. 64).

It is likewise true to say that it is only after adolescence that sexual development reaches the stage of what we may call "genetic" sexuality. Like physical and emotional love, the genital and psychic phases of sexuality should gradually be integrated into and subordinated to the highest and properly human expression of sexuality. Ideally, this occurs when a man and a woman give themselves to each other in the friendship-love that should characterize the married state. We call it "genetic" sexuality (from the word "genesis") because it is creative; indeed, according to Christian teaching the very purpose of the sex act as a biological function is procreation. Prior to this creative aspect, however, is the reciprocal gift love between a man and a woman, for whom the marital act is a concrete expression of their mutual love. In fact, we need not hesitate to say that the loftiest type of friendship is found in the mutual generous love of a husband and wife. We shall develop this further when we speak of marital and celibate love.

There is yet another aspect to the creative function of genetic sexuality. It is called by various names: sublimation (Freud), transformation (Neal Miller), transference (Joseph Nuttin), and psychiatrists differ in their explanation of the psychological process involved. For our purposes it suffices to draw some conclusions from the principles we have already stated. At the outset, we reject the theory of Kinsey, which is based almost exclusively on physiology, on genital sexuality, and on techniques of sexual activity. We are also cautious in accepting the teaching of Freud, who seems to have interpreted sublimation as a somewhat pathological process of displacement or transformation of sexual energy. The fact remains, however, that it is possible to sublimate or transfer sexual energy to activities on a higher level, such as artistic creativity, works of charity, higher studies or professional specialization. It can even be transferred, consciously or unconsciously, to such activities as sports, recreation or manual labor; and this is sometimes done in order to drain off the sexual energy in a "safe" area. Finally, psychologists also admit the possibility of sexual fetishism, as when an individual satisfies his sexual need by collecting women's shoes or underclothing. But this is not sublimation; it is a pathological perversion in which the sexual urge is directed to something other than the normal and proper sexual object.

The sexual urge is experienced as a need that seeks satisfaction and it is accompanied by a state of psychic tension. It has been verified that the tension can be relieved by a substitute satisfaction on the sensate level, and this method is effective in regard to most psychosomatic needs. This, however, is not sublimation of the sexual energy; it is a substitution or transference, as when an individual represses the sexual urge and finds sensate gratification in the intemperate use of food or drink. This may be done consciously and deliberately, but in many cases people do this without realizing it and they are surprised or indignant when someone tells them that they are intemperate.

Returning to our division of sexuality into genital, psychic and genetic, we would restrict the concept of "sublimation" to the genetic or creative level. Substitution and transference, as we have seen, can and do occur on all three levels, but since sublimation is a deliberate process by which one rises above the instincts and body needs, it requires the intervention of reason. At first glance it would seem to be an ideal way to pacify the tension that arises from the demands of our psychosomatic needs, such as the desire for some sort of sensate pleasure. And perhaps this is the way that most people would think of sublimation. But Benedict Groeschel points out that sublimation can also be "a subtle form of isolation" whereby a person avoids intimate human relationships. "There is often a tendency for the religiously motivated to hide from intimacy in some great cause or work. . . . Whatever the cause, it is better to be involved than to be hidden at home or in a disco, serving self. But it is wise to keep in mind that despite the legitimacy of the cause, some of the zeal may be a flight from real relationships and growth" (*Spiritual Passages*, p. 50). We shall have more to say about this when we treat of celibate love and sexuality. For the time being it suffices to say that while substitution, transference or sublimation are helpful techniques for those who as yet have little or no control over their sensate desires and physical urges, they are something quite different from the control that is exercised by mature persons through the virtue of temperance.

2

THE LOVE THAT IS CHARITY

When the psychologist speaks of love he is referring to one or all of the three types of human love: physical, emotional or volitional love. When the theologian speaks of the love that is charity, however, he must start with God and not with the human being, because charity is a divine love, a gift from God, a theological virtue infused by God. That is the way St. John describes it:

> Beloved, let us love one another because love is of God; everyone who loves is begotten of God and has knowledge of God.

> The man without love has known nothing of God, for God is love.

> God's love was revealed in our midst in this way: he sent his only Son to the world that we might have life through him.

> Love, then, consists in this: not that we have loved God but that he has loved us and has sent his Son as an offering for our sins.

> Beloved, if God has loved us so, we must have the same love for one another.

No one has ever seen God. Yet if we love one another, God dwells in us, and his love is brought to perfection in us. . . .

We, for our part, love because he first loved us. . . . The commandment we have from him is this: whoever loves God must also love his brother (1 Jn 4:7-21, *passim*).

We must not, therefore, begin a discussion of charity with our love for God or of our experience of God. Rather, as C.S. Lewis has stated, "We must begin at the real beginning, with love as the divine energy. This primal love is gift-love. In God there is no hunger that needs to be filled, only plenteousness that desires to give. The doctrine that God was under no necessity to create is not a piece of dry scholastic speculation. It is essential" (*The Four Loves*, p. 175).

Yet God's love is itself creative. Hence the enigmatic statement: we love things because they are good, but things are good because God loves them. The reason is that God does not love as we do. When we discover good in anything, that goodness evokes our love, but God's love creates the goodness in things. St. Thomas Aquinas explains this as follows: "When God wills things distinct from himself for the sake of his own goodness, it follows that it is his goodness alone that moves his will. Just as he understands things distinct from himself by gazing at his own essence, so also he wills things distinct from himself by willing his own goodness" (*Summa Theologiae*, I, 19, 2).

As a matter of fact, God's love cannot be dependent on the goodness in created things nor can he love those things in and for themselves. That would subordinate God to creatures. His love is therefore not an effect that follows upon his awareness of a created good; rather, it is the cause of that goodness. "God's love," says St. Thomas, "pours out and creates goodness in things" (*S.T.*, I, 20, 2). Moreover, since there is more goodness in some things than in others, it follows that God loves some more than others (cf. *S.T.*, I, 19, 3).

Charity and Merit

A number of conclusions can be drawn from the teaching of Sacred Scripture and theology. First, as we have just stated, the love that is charity is a gift from God and not simply the perfection of human love that is achieved by our own efforts. Secondly, charity is a sharing in the divine love by which God loves himself and all that he has created. For that reason St. Therese of Lisieux could write: "In order to love you as you loved me, I have to borrow your very own love"; and St. Thomas Aquinas said: "The charity by which we love our neighbor in a supernatural manner is a participation in divine charity." Thirdly, there is no terminus or limit to the love that is charity; since it is a supernatural and divine love, it is not subject to the limitations of our human nature. St. Augustine is said to have exclaimed: "O God, you give me the grace to love you, and when I love you, you give me the grace to love you more!" Finally, although Christ gave us a twofold precept of charity — love of God and love of neighbor — there is only one love by which we love all that we love through charity. We are commanded to love everything in and for God, because "it is impossible," says St. Augustine, "to fragment charity."

Charity is described by the theologians as a supernatural virtue or power that is infused in us together with the gift of sanctifying grace. It is first received through the sacrament of baptism, either baptism of water or baptism of desire. Moreover, it is Catholic teaching that we can merit an increase of grace and charity through good works that are performed in the state of grace and are properly motivated. Yet, in a strict sense, we cannot merit anything supernatural. When God rewards our good works he is really doing so, as St. Augustine says, on the basis of his free gift of grace. In this respect we are like the good and industrious servants who were rewarded by their master because they made a profit on the money he gave them in the first place (Mt 25:14-30).

And speaking of merit, it is encouraging to realize that merit does not depend only on the good work that is done but also on the motive and manner of doing it. It is not so much what we do, but the love with which we do it. St. Augustine, St. John of the Cross, St. Teresa of Avila and St. Catherine of Siena are some of the spiritual masters who have taught that a small work or deed performed with intense love may be much more meritorious than a great work performed with less love or for an imperfect motive. This should be a great consolation and encouragement for those Christians who, faithful to the duties of their state of life, nevertheless feel that their lives and works are insignificant. What, after all, was the daily life of the Blessed Virgin Mary, a housewife, and that of St. Joseph, a carpenter?

This same teaching also provides an answer to the question of whether the more difficult tasks and works are more meritorious. St. Thomas Aquinas raised this same question, and he responds as follows: "In determining the basis of merit and virtue, the good is much more important than the difficult. Therefore it does not follow that whatever is more difficult is more meritorious, but only that which, besides being more difficult, is also better" (*Summa Theologiae*, II-II, 27, 8, ad 3). He does admit, however, that sometimes the more difficult work may be more meritorious because it requires a more intense act of love, but the merit is determined by the love rather than the difficulty.

But if the intensity of love is so important, what can we say of those actions that are performed with less love, for example, with lukewarmness or simply out of a sense of duty? This is a problem that has vexed many theologians: the problem of the so-called "remiss" acts. It is closely related to the debated question concerning the morality of voluntary imperfections. As regards the merit of actions that are performed with less intense love than that of which we are capable, perhaps it is best to say that since those actions are good, not evil, they are meritorious and they do serve to keep one in the state of sanctifying grace. As regards voluntary imperfections, although some actions may be so imperfect as to constitute a venial sin, in principle we should make a distinction between venial sin and voluntary imperfections. There may be extenuating circumstances in the performance of a remiss action; moreover, an imperfect act does not cease to be good simply because it is imperfect. We must not brand the less good as evil and sinful. A lesser good is not necessarily evil and, equally important, a lesser evil is not good.

The Virtue of Charity

Coming back to the love which is charity, it would seem that it transcends human love to such an extent that somehow they are in opposition to each other. But such is not the case; the only love that is in any way contrary to charity is sinful love. We have already seen that both self-centered love (need-love) and generous friendship love (gift-love) are part of our human nature. As such, they have been implanted in us by our Creator, and therefore they are basically good. As long as they are subordinated to reason enlightened by faith they will never be sinful.

Moreover, as St. Thomas Aquinas teaches, the supernatural order of grace and charity does not destroy human nature; it works through it to perfect it (cf. *Summa Theologiae*, I, 1, 8, ad 2). Consequently, our next task is to discover which human love — need-love or generous love — is most properly the vehicle for the divine love that is charity. In a certain sense, however, the love that is charity transcends all distinctions such as need-love, gift-love, love of desire and benevolent love. Just as sanctifying grace elevates us to the status of children of God, sharing in his very nature and life, so also the virtue of charity divinizes human love and makes it an instrument or channel of divine love. Further, since the highest form of human love is volitional or friendship love — the only love that can be totally generous — it would seem most appropriate to identify that love with the virtue of charity. Such is the teaching of St. Thomas Aquinas:

> Since there is a certain sharing of something between man and God, so far as he shares his happiness with us, it is fitting that a friendship be based on this sharing. Concerning this sharing, First Corinthians states: "God is faithful, and it was he who called you to fellowship with his Son, Jesus Christ our Lord" (1 Cor 1:9). But the love that is based on this fellowship is charity. Therefore it is clear that charity is friendship between man and God (*Summa Theologiae*, II-II, 23, 1).

One must be careful, however, not to exalt the transcendence of charity to such a degree as to be reluctant to allow for any form of self-centered need-love or even to question whether it is proper to love oneself with the virtue of charity. The answer is readily at hand. We read in Sacred Scripture, in both the Old and the New Testaments, that we are to love our neighbor *as we love ourselves* (cf. Dt 6:5; Lv 19:18; Mt 22:37-40). Hence, the origin or starting point for love of neighbor is love of self; and it is also the modality of friendship: to love and treat the other as we want to be loved and treated. But, says St. Thomas, "the reason for which we love our neighbor is God, since what we should love in our neighbor is that he may be in God" (*Summa Theologiae*, II-II, 25, 1, ad 1).

At this point we can read with profit the observations of

two modern theologians who have written about charity in a masterly fashion, but each with his own explanation of the place of need-love and gift-love in the virtue of charity. First of all we have a lengthy quotation from Bernard Haring:

> The so-called love of desire (*love of concupiscence*) is genuine love, if in the object loved, in the *value-for-me*, one recognizes at least obscurely the *value-in-itself* and takes pleasure in it. Once man realizes that only God can make him happy, that he is ordered utterly and entirely to God, and accordingly begins to sacrifice everything which proves an obstacle to his effort to seek his happiness in God, then he already has true love even though at direct first blush it is no more than the movement of love of desire. Yet the perfect form of love is love of friendship (*love of benevolence*). Possessed of this love, one rejoices over the value of another for his own sake, exults over him, has the desire to attest his love and esteem for him and in every way show him respect and honor.

> On the supernatural plane, love of desire corresponds to the divine virtue of hope, whereas the love of benevolence [friendship love] corresponds to the virtue of love [charity]. Supernatural hope is that undreamed-of fulfillment of the Greek (Platonic) *Eros* on the highest level of the ideal, the loftiest flight of yearning and aspiring love, which knows no rest until it has ascended to the divine. And yet supernatural hope is essentially distinct from the Greek *Eros*, for it does not spring from man himself but from the gracious and un-merited bounty and condescension of God. . . . It cannot be the flight of mere man, no matter how lofty his desire (*The Law of Christ*, Vol. II, pp. 87-88).

Our second quotation comes from the well-known Anglican theologian, C.S. Lewis, who has written so profoundly on the subject of human love and charity:

But in addition to these natural loves God can bestow a far better gift; or rather, since our minds must divide and pigeon-hole, two gifts.

He communicates to men a share of his own gift-love. This is different from the gift-loves he has built into their nature. . . . Divine gift-love is wholly disinterested and desires what is simply best for the beloved. . . . That such a gift-love comes by grace and should be called charity, everyone will agree. But I have to add something which will not perhaps be so easily admitted. God, as it seems to me, bestows two other gifts: a supernatural need-love of himself and a supernatural need-love of one another. . . . All the activities (sins only excepted) of the natural loves can in a favored hour become works of the glad and shameless and grateful need-love or of the selfless, unofficious gift-love, which are both charity (*The Four Loves*, pp. 177-184, *passim*).

The excellence of charity as a virtue should be evident from the fact that St. Paul has stated: "Now I will show you the way which surpasses all the others. If I speak with human tongues and angelic as well, but do not have love, I am a noisy gong, a clanging cymbal. If I have the gift of prophecy and, with full knowledge, comprehend all mysteries, if I have faith great enough to move mountains, but have not love, I am nothing. If I give everything I have to feed the poor and hand over my body to be burned, but have not love, I gain nothing. . . . There are in the end three things that last: faith, hope and love, and the greatest of these is love" (1 Cor 13:1-3; 13).

Charity and Holiness

Not only is charity the most excellent of all the Christian virtues; it is also the principal and most essential element of

Christian holiness and perfection. The virtue of faith puts us in
contact with God as the source of divine truth; the virtue of hope
enables us to move towards God as our ultimate end and the
source of our eternal happiness; but the virtue of charity is the
friendship love that establishes our bond of union with God,
who is infinite goodness. It is said, therefore, that the Christian
life ends where it begins: in love. And St. John of the Cross has
stated: "In the evening of life you will be judged by love."

Theologians make a distinction in the activity of the infused virtues, including charity. For example, an act of obedience performed precisely as an act of obedience is an "elicited"
act of that virtue. An act of obedience performed by reason of the
vow of obedience is an elicited act of obedience that is "commanded" by the virtue of religion. If done for the love of God,
then the acts of both of these virtues are commanded by the
virtue of charity. This is simply another way of explaining why
the virtue of charity is the principal element in Christian perfection and should direct the acts of all the other virtues to their
proper end. Even on the natural level, of course, love is the
springboard of all our actions.

We have stated previously that there is no terminus to
grace and charity; they can increase indefinitely. That being the
case, there must be degrees or grades of Christian perfection,
since all growth admits of stages of development. These stages
or grades of perfection have been described traditionally as
purgative, illuminative and unitive. But St. Thomas Aquinas
uses the ancient terminology: beginners, advanced and perfect.
Thus, St. Augustine states in his commentary on the First Letter
of John: "As soon as charity is born, it takes food; after taking
food, it waxes strong; and when it has become strong, it is
perfected." This division is more closely related to the virtue of
charity, as we see in the teaching of St. Thomas Aquinas:

The various degrees of charity are distinguished according to the various pursuits to which man is brought by the increase of charity. At first it is incumbent on man to occupy himself chiefly with avoiding sin and resisting his sensate desires, which move him in opposition to charity. This concerns *beginners*, in whom charity has to be fed or fostered lest it be destroyed.

In the second place, man's chief pursuit is to aim at progress in good, as this is the pursuit of the *advanced*, whose chief aim is to strengthen their charity by adding to it.

Man's third pursuit is to aim chiefly at union with and enjoyment of God, and this belongs to the *perfect*, who desire to be dissolved and to be with Christ (*Summa Theologiae*, II-II, 24, 9).

Later on, when treating of the universal call to perfection for all Christians, after stating that the perfection of the Christian life consists in charity, St. Thomas explains the three ways in which we may talk about perfection:

The first is absolute perfection, which implies a totality not only on the part of the lover but also on the part of the one loved, so that God is loved to the extent that he is lovable. Such perfection is not possible for any creature but is proper to God alone, in whom goodness is found integrally and essentially.

Another perfection consists in the absolute totality on the part of the lover, so that his love always tends actually to God in its full capacity. Such a perfection is not possible to man on earth, but will be possible in heaven.

But a third perfection does not require a totality as regards the lovableness of the beloved or the capacity of the lover in the sense that one is always actually loving God, but it excludes everything that would be contrary to the movement of love for God. . . . Such perfection is possible in this life, and in two ways. First, so far as everything incompatible with charity, i.e., mortal sin, is excluded from the will of a man. Without this type of perfection, charity cannot exist, and hence it is necessary for salvation. Secondly, so far as the will of a man rejects not only what is incompatible with charity, but even that which would prevent the affection of the soul from being directed totally to God. Charity can exist without this perfection, for example, in the beginners and in the advanced (S.T. II-II, 184, 2).

At first glance it would seem that St. Thomas Aquinas requires very little for the perfection of charity. Indeed, one may be tempted to conclude from the above quotation that it suffices for Christian perfection to avoid mortal sin and to live habitually in the state of grace. Such, however, is not a correct application of the precept of charity, which is found, as we have already seen, in the Old and New Testaments. We are commanded to strive for that perfection of charity whereby we love the Lord our God with our whole heart and soul, mind and strength. In other words, we have as our ideal to live the totality of love which is the state, not of the beginners or advanced souls, but the state of the perfect. And the fact that numerous Christians never reach this high state of perfection does not nullify the universal vocation to the perfection of charity nor does it mean that its attainment is an extraordinary, charismatic gift given to the few.

The Second Vatican Council, in its "Dogmatic Constitution on the Church" (*Lumen Gentium*) states without any qualification: "All the faithful, whatever their condition or state — though each in his or her own way — are called by the Lord to that perfection of sanctity by which the Father himself is perfect" (LG, 11). The same teaching is repeated later on in the same document: "It is therefore quite clear that all Christians in any state or walk of life are called to the fullness of Christian life and to the perfection of charity, and by this holiness a more human manner of life is fostered also in earthly society. . . . The forms and tasks of life are many but holiness is one. . . . Each one, however, according to his or her own gifts and duties must steadfastly advance along the way of a living faith, which arouses hope and works through love" (LG, 40).

God, Self and Neighbor

The virtue of charity does not refer to God alone; we are also commanded to love our neighbor. That is what Christ gave to his disciples as a precept: to love God and to love their neighbor. If one of us had been present when Jesus gave that command, he or she might well have asked: "What about me, Lord? Do I have to give all my love to God and neighbor and leave nothing for myself?"

We can imagine that Christ would have responded more or less as follows: "Do I have to command you to love yourself? Is that not the first law of your nature, to love and desire good for yourself? And does it not frequently become an obstacle to your love of God and neighbor?" It is, in fact, a lifelong battle for some people and, as St. Alphonsus Liguori stated, it doesn't end until a few hours after they are dead!

Nevertheless, we should love ourselves with the love that is charity, if only because we were created for eternal happiness in heaven. Therefore we should desire for ourselves whatever will help us reach that glorious goal. As we have seen, C.S. Lewis readily admitted that "need-love" understood in that context is a gift from God and indeed an aspect of the virtue of charity. As such, it is not an obstacle to one's love of God and neighbor; rather, in desiring good for ourselves through the virtue of charity, we are actually seeking our own spiritual perfection and the glory of God.

From another point of view we could say that our love of self through charity connotes our indigence and our dependence on God as well as the recognition that it is in him alone that we can find complete happiness and perfection. Finally, since charity is friendship-love between God and the human person, it must be a mutual generous or benevolent love. But God's gift of love to us must also be accepted and acknowledged; indeed, in friendship the ability to receive love is as important as the ability to give love. There is, then, an order or a priority in the exercise of the love that is charity. We are commanded to love God above all things and with all our heart; hence, the primary object of charity is God himself. In and through God we love all that we love through charity. Secondly, as we have seen, we should love ourselves and, in fact, we are obliged to love our own spiritual good and ultimate salvation more than that of our neighbor. Hence, although prompted by love and concern for others, a person who is weak in a given virtue should never work in an apostolate in which he or she will be severely tempted to sin. We are obliged to avoid the proximate occasions of sin. In the third place we are commanded to love our neighbor, as was stated by Christ at the Last Supper: "I give you a new commandment: Love one another. Such as my love has been for you, so must your love be for each other. This is how all will know you for my disciples: your love for one another" (Jn 13:34-35). In his *Commentary on John*, St. Augustine puts it this way:

> Perhaps in loving your brother, you do so without loving Christ? How could this be possible, since those whom you love are the members of Christ? When you love the members of Christ, it is Christ whom you love. When you love the Son of God, it is the Father also whom you love. It is impossible to fragment charity. Choose whom you will love, and the rest will follow (*In Jn*, tr. 10, n. 33; PL 35).

St. Thomas Aquinas voices the same teaching: "The reason for which we love our neighbor is God. . . . Hence it is evident that the act by which we love God and the act by which we love our neighbors are of the same species. . . . The neighbor should be loved for what there is of God in him" (*Summa Theologiae*, II-II, 25, 1).

Here also there is a priority. Those who are closest to us, such as members of our own family, are more deserving of our love than those related to us by other ties. Yet the actual expression of charity in service to others should be determined by their need of our love and care. Christ himself frequently reminded his disciples to care for the poor, and throughout the history of Christianity the Church has always ministered to those in need.

More challenging, however, is the command to love our enemies. Early in his public ministry, in his Sermon on the Mount, Christ urged his listeners to strive for greater perfection in many areas of their life, including their love of others:

> You have heard the commandment: "You shall love your countryman but hate your enemy." My command to you is: love your enemies, pray for your persecutors. This will prove that you are sons of your heavenly Father, for his sun rises on the bad and the good, he rains on the just and the unjust. If you love those who love you, what merit is there in that? Do not tax collectors do as much? And if you greet your brothers only, what is so praiseworthy about that? Do not pagans do as much? In a word, you must be made perfect as your heavenly Father is perfect (Mt 5:43-48).

And who are our enemies? First of all our "persecutors," that is, those who do not love us, treat us uncharitably or actually wish us evil. Secondly, we could classify those persons as our "enemies" for whom we do not feel love, usually because there is something in their character or their actions that displeases us or makes it difficult for us to relate to them in a loving manner. On the purely human level some people are not very lovable and this causes tension and friction in human relations. But Christ urges us to love all our neighbors individually with the love that is charity, though not necessarily with the emotion of love by which we "like" certain individuals. St. Thomas Aquinas makes the following interesting observation concerning love of neighbor:

> A person is loved in two ways. Either he is loved for his own sake . . . or he is loved because of the friendship one has for another person. Thus, if you love someone, you will also love those who are connected with him — his children, his servants, and all those who relate to him in some way. It may happen that we will love a friend to such an extent that, for his sake, among those who are connected with him, we will love even those who have offended us or are hostile to us. This is the way our charity extends even to our enemies: we love them because of our love of God, to whom our love is primarily directed (*Summa Theologiae*, II-II, 23, 1, ad 2).

It is in this particular area that the virtue of prudence should determine our attitude and actions towards our "enemies." To go out to them with exuberant and affectionate signs of friendship would be insincere and pharisaical. It may even cause them to withdraw farther from us or be more hostile to us. We must be realistic and acknowledge that just as we are more drawn to some persons and can readily form a friendship with them, so also we may feel an aversion to some individuals, sometimes with good reason. Consequently, the prudent and Christian thing to do in their regard is to manifest the ordinary signs of politeness and to include them in our prayers.

We sometimes hear an objection raised in regard to love of

neighbor, whether friend or enemy, and it is this: Christians seem to "use" their neighbor. They love their neighbor in and for God, but not as an individual human person. Some may even base their objection on the teaching of Christ. "Why," they will ask, "do you always have to bring Christ into your love and care for others?" They find difficulty with Christ's parable concerning the last judgment. Those who inherit the kingdom ask: "Lord, when did we see you hungry and feed you or see you thirsty and give you drink? When did we welcome you away from home or clothe you in your nakedness? When did we visit you when you were ill or in prison?" And the king replies: "I assure you, as often as you did it for one of my least brothers, you did it for me" (cf. Mt 25:37-40).

Actually, this parable is the second stage of the teaching of Christ on love of neighbor. At first he had repeated the teaching of the Old Testament, which commanded the Jews to love their neighbor as themselves. It is another way of phrasing the Golden Rule of the ancients: "Do unto others as you would have them do unto you." But now Christ raises love of neighbor to a higher level, asking his followers to love their neighbor as they love Christ. He is the standard and measure of our love of neighbor; indeed, it is our love for Christ that makes it possible to love even our enemies. We love and serve others in Jesus' name.

From a theological point of view it is necessary to rise above the purely human level of love, even in its highest form, if we are to love others as Christians. As we have already seen, there is an essential difference between the infused, supernatural virtue of charity and the various degrees of human love. Not that the love that is charity annihilates all human love and affection, for St. Thomas Aquinas reminds us that "charity encloses within itself all human affections, except those which are based on sin and which, for this reason, cannot be directed to beatitude. That is why the affection which exists between relatives, fellow citizens, those who travel the same walk of life, and equals of any condition can be an object of merit and charity" (*De Caritate*, art. 7).

The teaching of Christ did not stop at the second level of charity — loving and serving others in his name — but in his discourse at the Last Supper he gave his followers the key to the perfection of charity. "This is my commandment: love one another as I have loved you" (Jn 15:12). Then, to reveal to them the extent of his love, Christ said: "There is no greater love than this: to lay down one's life for one's friends" (Jn 15:13).

To love others as Christ loved us, that is the perfection of charity. It is especially at this level of love that we see how much the love that is charity transcends natural human love. One who loves others in this way is loving them with Christ's own love just as surely as a person in the state of grace shares in the very nature and life of God. This is the love that we see in the saints and mystics, and because of this love, even their ordinary, insignificant works and actions were steps that led to a high degree of sanctity. The reason for this is that it is not what we do that makes us holy, but the love with which we do it. St. Augustine puts it this way:

> It seems to me that the briefest and most concise definition of virtue is to call it the order of love, since that is truly virtuous which gives all things their rightful share of love, loving them to the degree that each one deserves to be loved, and no more. . . . Therefore it is fitting to define temperance as the love of God keeping one entire and incorrupt; fortitude as love readily enduring all things for God; justice, serving God alone and thereby rightly ordering the things that pertain to men; prudence, correctly discerning those things that will lead to God and those that will impede progress to him (*De Moribus*, 15).

It is in that context that St. Augustine says: "Love God, and do what you will; you will not sin."

The Effects of Charity

Following the teaching of St. Thomas Aquinas, we have stated that the virtue of charity is a friendship-love; that is, a generous gift-love that goes out to the other, whether that other is God or neighbor. We have explained that the order of charity is first of all to love God above all things, then to love self in view of one's own perfection and ultimate happiness, and finally to love one's neighbor. However, when we speak of charity as friendship-love, we are concerned with only two objects — God and neighbor — since a person is not said to be a friend to himself or herself. Friendship requires at least two persons. But how shall we know whether or not we are truly exercising the virtue of charity in relation to God and neighbor? One way of knowing is to examine what we may call the psychological effects of the love that is charity; they are for the most part quite different from the effects of self-centered need-love. St. Thomas Aquinas discussed the effects of love at some length in the *Summa Theologiae*, I-II, q. 28, and we shall use his teaching as a framework for our comments.

Detachment. This particular effect of love is the first one that is experienced, although St. Thomas Aquinas uses the word "ecstasy" to designate it. By this he means that whether it be a question of the emotion of love or the volitional love of the will, a person will be carried outside himself toward the good that he loves. Thus, the ecstasy or transport of love bears some resemblance to the original meaning of erotic love (Eros). But in our day the words "ecstasy" and "erotic love" may be misleading, and for that reason it is better to speak of "transport of love" or "being drawn to the object of love."

The first movement of love is always toward that which is loved. The transport of love is experienced in both the passion of love and in friendship-love, but there is a vast difference between the two. The passion of love, like all the emotions, will begin and terminate in self. Therefore, says St. Thomas Aquinas, the person who experiences the emotion of love is truly transported to the object that is loved, but it is because "he is anxious to enjoy something which is as yet outside his grasp" and "he is anxious to have that other thing for himself." In friendship-love, on the other hand, the lover is "carried outside himself insofar as he wants and works for his friend's good" (*Summa Theologiae*, I-II, 28, 4). But in carrying the lover toward the beloved, the transport of friendship-love also detaches the lover from self and from anything that would be an obstacle to the movement toward the beloved. For that reason, we have opted to name "detachment" as the first effect of love. In a sense, however, transport and detachment are two sides of the same coin.

Psychologists speak of "the principle of reality," and by this they mean that if a person chooses one of two incompatible objects, he must give up the other. Thus, if a person decides to turn to the right, he cannot at the same time turn to the left. This is based on the philosophical "principle of contradiction": a thing cannot "be" and "not be" at the same time under the same aspect. We learn these principles from the experience of every-day life. Even in our childhood there were countless situations in which we had to choose one thing rather than another simply because we could not have both.

Applying these principles to the virtue of charity, we note first of all that the love that is charity can carry a person toward any one of the three objects of charity: God, self or neighbor. And immediately, to forestall any objections, we must assert that we have an obligation to love ourselves with the virtue of charity, if only because we have an obligation to strive for the perfection of charity. But this will necessarily involve a withdrawal from anything that is incompatible with or contrary to the good that is loved and the good that is desired for the beloved. Thus, Jesus said: "You cannot love God and mammon."

Choices have to be made, and when it is a question of the love that is charity, the choice is between loving for the sake of the other or loving exclusively for the sake of oneself. That is why St. Thomas Aquinas said that regardless of its name, every sin has its origin in self-centered love. Ultimately there are only two choices: love of other or love of self; and in circumstances in which one has an obligation to act out of love of God or neighbor, one has to relinquish self-love.

Sin is the only thing that can impede or destroy the virtue of charity, and therefore the first requirement for living the Christian life and for growth in holiness is to put sin out of one's life and to avoid all proximate occasions of sin. This is the function of detachment, which is called by various names — asceticism, mortification, self-denial, purgation — but in every case it requires that the Christian detach himself or herself from anything that is an obstacle to the love of God and neighbor.

This particular stage of the spiritual life, as we have mentioned, is called the purgative stage, although self-denial and purification are necessary even in the higher stages. St. John of the Cross is universally regarded as one of the greatest authorities on this topic, especially in his treatises, the *Ascent of Mount Carmel* and *The Dark Night of the Soul*. There are, of course, numerous books and articles that treat of the ascetical practices of self-denial and purification but many of them deal only with the avoidance of sin and temptation. St. John of the Cross gets to the very core of the matter, namely, the purgation of our selfish desires:

> We are not treating here of the lack of things, since this implies no detachment on the part of the soul if it has a desire for them; but we are treating of the detachment from them of

the taste and desire, for it is this that leaves the soul free and void of them, although it may have them; for it is not the things of this world that either occupy the soul or cause it harm, since they enter it not, but rather the will and desire for them, for it is these that dwell within it. . . .

The affection and attachment which the soul has for creatures renders the soul like to these creatures; and, the greater is its affection, the closer is the equality and likeness between them; for love creates a likeness between that which loves and that which is loved. . . . And thus, he that loves a creature becomes as low as that creature and, in some ways, lower; for love not only makes the lover equal to the object of his love, but even subjects him to it. . . .

It is true that all the desires are not equally hurtful. . . . I am speaking of those desires that are voluntary, for the natural desires hinder the soul little, if at all, from attaining to union, as long as they are not consented to or do not pass beyond the first movements . . ., and to take away these — that is, to mortify them wholly in this life — is impossible. . . . But all the other voluntary desires, whether they be of mortal sin, which are the gravest, or of venial sin, which are less grave, or whether they be only of imperfections, which are the least grave of all, must be driven away every one, and the soul must be free from them all, howsoever slight they be, if it is to come to this complete union (*Ascent of Mount Carmel*, I, 3, 4; 4, 3; 11, 2).

Union. All love seeks union with the person or thing that is loved. Selfish love, also called the love of desire, will seek union in order to possess, to receive something for self; generous friendship love will seek union in order to give to the beloved. There is, in fact, a mutual giving of self, as in an ideal Christian marriage. But in every case the terminus of the transport of love is union with the person or object loved.

We have already observed that even the emotion of love, which is basically self-centered, tends toward physical nearness and union with the object of that love. The same thing is true of human friendship; that is why separation or absence from one's friends causes a unique kind of suffering. Consequently, since charity is also a type of love, it will necessarily tend toward union with the object of charity. Because of our natural tendency to believe in the existence of God, some theologians go so far as to say that it is, as it were, "natural" to desire intimate union with him. This is surely the case with those who already love God. Not that in this life we can see God or enjoy his divine friendship to the fullest. St. Teresa of Avila has stated: "I want to see God; but to see God I must die"; and St. Augustine affirmed that our hearts are restless until they rest in God.

But how is it possible for us in this life actually to achieve union with God? We cannot do it by our own efforts, that is certain. "The good that God has promised us," says St. Thomas Aquinas, "so exceeds our nature that, far from being able to attain it, our natural faculties could never suspect it or desire it" (*De Veritate*, 14, 2). It is God who makes the first move, and he does so by infusing sanctifying grace into the soul. By means of that grace the individual is reborn as a child of God. St. Peter proclaims this in the following words: "Praised be the God and Father of our Lord Jesus Christ, he who in his great mercy gave us new birth; a birth unto hope which draws its life from the resurrection of Jesus Christ from the dead; a birth to an imperishable inheritance, incapable of fading or defilement, which is kept in heaven for you who are guarded with God's power through faith; a birth to a salvation which stands ready to be revealed in the last days" (1 P 1:3-5).

Thus, through the gift of sanctifying grace, we are united with God to such a degree that we share in the very nature and life of God (cf. 2 P 1:4). Sanctifying grace makes our nature divine, as it were, but it does not destroy our nature. Not only that, but together with sanctifying grace we receive the whole array of the supernatural, infused virtues and the gifts of the Holy Spirit. Hence, even a newly baptized infant receives all that is needed ultimately to arrive at the transforming union of the mystical state. It is on the basis of this that we can speak of the universal vocation to perfection, meaning that every Christian is called to the perfection of charity.

God first loved us, as St. John says (1 Jn 4:10), and he established friendship with us through the gift of his grace. But friendship requires a mutual love; it calls for a response on the part of the one who is loved. Once again it is St. John who tells us: "We, for our part, love because he first loved us. . . . The love of God consists in this: that we keep his commandments — and his commandments are not burdensome" (1 Jn 4:19; 5:3; cf. also 1 Cor 13:4-13). This brings to mind the statement of St. Augustine: "Love God and do what you will; you will not sin."

True friendship requires that the two friends strive to achieve perfect conformity and identification of their wills if they are to experience the unity that is the fruit of love. Charles Heris puts it this way:

> When two friends have united their lives to the point that they have the same plans, the same ambitions, the same desires, they have attained the perfection of friendship and experienced the joy of being one in their love.

> Now charity, here below, can arrive at that identification of ourselves with God; it requires only the constant fulfillment of the divine will. What is more, it tends to this of its very nature. The fulfillment of God's will is not always perfect, however, because our weakness causes obstacles. But what is required is that our will be constantly aimed at union with God's will. This union is easy, for if we will the good of God, God also wills our good, which is himself. And since the will is one of our most intimate powers, while God's will *is* God,

when our will is in union with the divine will, we are united with God in the most intimate part of our being. Eternity can do no more than stamp its final seal upon this mutual union in the act of love (*Spirituality of Love*, p. 129).

We are commanded to love God above all things and to love our neighbor as Christ loved us. St. John insists, therefore, that our love of God and union with him by conforming our wills to his must be the origin and source of love and union with our fellow Christians. "The way we came to understand love was that he laid down his life for us. . . . Let us love in deed and in truth and not merely talk about it. . . . Beloved, if God has loved us so, we must have the same love for one another. No one has ever seen God. Yet, if we love one another, God dwells in us, and his love is brought to perfection in us" (1 Jn 3:16-4:12, *passim*).

Joy. In years gone by, the little child in religion class would be asked: "Why did God make you?" Immediately the child would recite the answer memorized from the catechism: "God made me to know him, to love him and to serve him in this life and be happy with him forever in heaven."

Centuries ago, St. Thomas Aquinas asked the same question: why did God create human beings? And he gave the same answer as was given by the child: God created human beings for eternal happiness in heaven. "By nature," says St. Thomas, "the creature endowed with reason wishes to be happy and therefore cannot wish not to be happy" (*Contra Gentes*, 4, 92). And the poet Wordsworth said: "Trailing clouds of glory, we come from God who is our home." In fact, we can already have a foretaste of the happiness and joy of heaven if our love of God carries us to union with him.

Josef Pieper asserts that "all love has joy as its natural fruit. What is more, all human happiness . . . is fundamentally *the happiness of love*" (*About Love*, p. 72). The truth of this statement is evident even from a consideration of the emotion of love. The three pleasure emotions are listed as love, desire and joy. When an individual is attracted to a sensate good, love is stimulated. If the love is intense enough, it will give rise to a desire for the good in question. Finally, if one succeeds in obtaining the good, he experiences the joy or satisfaction of possessing it. The joy that proceeds from love and desire is a fact of everyday experience as is, conversely, the sadness that is the result of unrequited love and unfulfilled desires. Hence, St. Thomas states that "both joy and sadness have their origin in love, though in quite contrary ways" (*Summa Theologiae*, II-II, 28, 1).

Spiritual joy is the effect of the virtue of charity, and St. Thomas Aquinas distinguishes two kinds of joy in the Lord: first, to rejoice in divine goodness simply because it is what it is; second, to rejoice in the fact that we share in the divine goodness (through sanctifying grace, the supernatural virtues and the gifts of the Holy Spirit). Of these two kinds of joy, the first is the better and is a special effect of the virtue of charity, whereas the second kind of joy proceeds also from the virtue of hope, whereby we look forward to full enjoyment of God's goodness (cf. *Summa Theologiae*, II-II, 28, 1 and 2).

Unfortunately, in the early centuries of the Christian epoch some of the Fathers, like Origen who wrote a commentary on the Song of Songs, were so fearful of yielding to carnal desires that they consciously or unconsciously promulgated a doctrine that is totally alien to joy in the Christian life. The seeds that they had sown came to full bloom with the Jansenists in France in the seventeenth century, of whom Ronald Knox said: "Jansenism never learned to smile" (*Enthusiasm*, p. 212). The same negative spirituality is prevalent today in some parts of the Christian world, with the result that holiness of life is equated with scrupulosity and melancholy. The motto of such Christians seems to be that whatever gives pleasure is sinful. Walter Farrell, however, gives us a truer and more optimistic picture:

The circulation of pictures of dyspeptic looking saints was one of the master strokes of satanic propaganda. Certainly this contributed no little to the modern notion that saints are a sour, grumpy lot. Nothing could be further from the truth. The saints are always great lovers; and love floods our hearts with the sunshine of joy, particularly when the love is for a divine friend. Look at it objectively for a moment. This unselfish love has identified our will with the will of our Friend; his happiness is ours, even as it is between human friends. From the first moment of this divine friendship, our Friend is always and intimately with us. . . . Nothing can threaten his happiness; nothing can dim the joy of our friendship.

This is the pervading influence behind all Christian life: where there is charity, there is joy. And where there is joy, life can be lived intensely, merrily. . . . Charity, you will remember, is the common heritage of every Christian in the state of grace, of everyone who is a friend of God. It is not only the saints who live merrily, but the humblest of men with the least degree of charity (*A Companion to the Summa*, vol. III, pp. 97-98).

Zeal. This quality is defined in the dictionary as enthusiastic and diligent devotion in pursuit of a cause, ideal or goal; also, fervent adherence or service. That describes perfectly what we mean by zeal as an effect of the gift-love that is charity. It is worth noting, however, that St. Thomas Aquinas provides an interesting distinction concerning zeal, depending on whether it follows upon concupiscible (self-centered) love or friendship love:

Zeal, in whatever sense one takes the term, arises from the intensity of love. . . . Since therefore love is an active power bent upon the object loved . . . , an intense love will strive to resist anything opposed to it. But this works out differently in concupiscible love and in friendship love.

In the case of concupiscible love, a person who desires something intensely will react against anything that might impede the attainment or peaceful enjoyment of that which he loves. In this way a husband is said to be jealous of his wife, lest her association with others may jeopardize his singular and exclusive relationship with her. Similarly, those who strive for excellence may react against those who are already successful, seeing them as obstacles to their own advancement. . . .

Friendship love, however, seeks the good of one's friend, and when it is intense, it causes one to react against anything that may be detrimental to that good. Accordingly, one is said to be zealous in regard to a friend when he strives to fend off anything said or done against the friend's interests. In this way also one is said to be zealous concerning the things of God when he strives to the best of his ability to prevent anything that would be contrary to the honor or the will of God. Thus, Scripture says: "I have been most zealous for the Lord, the God of hosts" (1 K 19:14) (*Summa Theologiae*, I-II, 28, 4).

The distinction made by St. Thomas is necessary in order to avoid the extreme position of one author, who stated: "Where jealousy is felt, even the slightest shade, then the reputed love of another is merely love of self." We have already demonstrated that there is such a thing as a morally good love of self; indeed, as St. Thomas points out, "our love for ourselves is the model and root of friendship, for our friendship for others consists precisely in the fact that our attitude to them is the same as to ourselves." Consequently, "among all those things that relate to God and are loved out of charity, a man also loves himself out of charity" (*Summa Theologiae*, II-II, 25, 4). There is, therefore, a place for zeal or jealousy even in friendship love, and especially in marital and parental love.

The determining factor regarding the zeal or jealousy that is the effect of love will be the intensity of that love. The more intense one's love for another, the greater the zeal in combatting every obstacle or impediment to that love. Of course, it is likewise true that an excessive self-love will turn zeal into jealousy and envy. We then witness a jealousy that is destructive instead of a jealousy or zeal that is protective and supportive of the beloved. Yet even here there is always the danger of an over-protective zeal that smothers the individual and makes him or her excessively dependent on the lover. Such was the case of Mrs. Fidget, described by C.S. Lewis in *The Four Loves* (pp. 48-50). Her family had no rest from her ministrations until she herself was laid to rest.

In the Christian life, zeal for the things of God will prompt one to a conscientious observance of God's laws, much as the intense love of a mother for her children will prompt her to the conscientious performance of the duties of her state in life, or the love of a pastor for his parishioners will prompt him to a life of dedicated service. It is the same zeal of charity that has stimulated the great preachers, missionaries, teachers and saintly bishops throughout the history of the Church. The zeal that flows from the intense love of God and neighbor is the seed of the evangelical activity of the People of God.

Sacrifice. Wherever there is intense gift-love, there is zeal for the beloved; and wherever there is zeal for the beloved, there is a spirit of sacrifice. We have already discussed detachment as a first fruit of gift-love, and that necessarily involves self-denial; but sacrifice implies much more. All generous love of another necessarily demands some degree of detachment from anything that would be contrary to gift-love. Hence, "in order to find favor with the beloved, a lover will make himself humble and submissive to his service. He will respect his least desires and make every effort to satisfy them. His whole being will be in harmony with his beloved, without ever using the loved one to satisfy his own caprices. . . . Such a love safeguards the dignity of the person loved: he remains a goal in himself, toward which the lover directs his affection and to whom he submits as to a person who does not belong to him but constantly proclaims his otherness" (C.V. Heris, *Spirituality of Love*, p. 103). All this runs counter to the egotistic, self-centered love that tempts one to use the other for one's own interests, utility or pleasure.

Fortunately, the human heart is capable of a devotion and spirit of sacrifice that transcend all self-centered interest. This is realized when the good of the beloved surpasses everything else. Such a disinterested love is exemplified in the young woman who forfeits marriage, home and family in order to dedicate herself to an apostolate of charity; in the zealous layman who deprives himself of a high salary and a comfortable life in order to serve the People of God in the local church; in the policeman or soldier who sacrifice their very life in the line of duty.

Even the great saints and mystics were called upon by God to make sacrifices that were painful and repugnant to our self-centered love. Take the case of St. Therese of Lisieux, who has been judged by some to have been a sentimental, pampered young nun. Yet the truth of the matter is that almost from the time she entered Carmel, God laid on her the terrible cross of agonizing doubts against the virtue of faith. She was truly "a victim of merciful love" and in spite of the temptations to despair, she was able to murmur at the moment of her death: "My God, I love you!" It is well to remember that her full religious name was Therese of the Child Jesus and the Holy Face.

And so we end where we began, with the words of Jesus, commanding us to take up our cross daily and follow him. Perfect gift-love is exemplified always on the cross of Jesus crucified, who laid down his life for his friends. Hence, St. Teresa of Avila could exclaim: "To suffer or to die!"

The wisdom of the world is exactly opposed to the teachings of the Sermon on the Mount. Jesus says: blessed are the pure; the world says: blessed are they who indulge in loose living; Jesus says: blessed are those who weep; the world says: blessed are those who laugh and amuse themselves; Jesus says: blessed are the meek, the merciful; the world says: blessed are those who impose themselves on others and dominate them; Jesus says: blessed are the poor; the world says: blessed are the rich; Jesus says: blessed are those who suffer; the world says: blessed are those who enjoy themselves. We must come back to the Sermon on the Mount. We must not be afraid to say what Jesus said and to affirm it after him. The Beatitudes are preached too little (Francois Jamart, *I Believe in Love*, p. 126).

3

MARITAL LOVE

Christian marriage, when lived fully, offers a truly marvelous synthesis of all the loves that can engage the heart of man (C.V. Heris, *Spirituality of Love*, p. 183). It is, moreover, the "natural" vocation for every man and woman, since we read in Genesis that God said: "It is not good for the man to be alone. I will make a suitable partner for him" (Gn 2:18). Hence, as Walter Farrell pointed out, "marriage existed before sin came into the world; it exists after sin, not as a product of evil, but as a remedy against sin and a means to holiness" (*Companion to the Summa*, Vol. 4, p. 403). St. Thomas Aquinas asserts that "there obviously exists the greatest friendship between man and wife; they are united not only in the conjugal act, which . . . can produce a sweet and tender friendship; they are joined even more in their common sharing in the whole of family life" (*Summa Contra Gentiles*, III, q. 233).

Two other lengthy quotations from contemporary sources also emphasize the friendship-love that should characterize Christian marriage. The first is taken from the document on the Church in the modern world, issued by the Second Vatican Council and promulgated by Pope Paul VI on December 7, 1965:

Married love is an eminently human love because it is an affection between two persons rooted in the will and it embraces the good of the whole person; it can enrich the sentiments of the spirit and their physical expression with a unique dignity and ennoble them as the special elements and signs of the friendship proper to marriage. . . .

Endowed by mutual fidelity and, above all, consecrated by Christ's sacrament, this love abides faithfully in mind and body in prosperity and adversity and hence excludes both adultery and divorce. The unity of marriage, distinctly recognized by our Lord, is made clear in the equal personal dignity which must be accorded to man and wife in mutual and unreserved affection (*Gaudium et Spes*, n. 49).

The second quotation is taken from the Apostolic Exhortation issued by Pope John Paul II on November 22, 1981, under the title *Familiaris Consortio*. This document was written in response to the request of the Bishops' Synod on the family, held in Rome from September 26 to October 25, 1980:

The family, which is founded and given life by love, is a community of persons: of husband and wife, of parents and children, of relatives. Its first task is to live with fidelity the reality of communion in a constant effort to develop an authentic community of persons.

The inner principle of that task, its permanent power and its final goal is love: without love the family is not a community of persons and, in the same way, *without love the family cannot live, grow and perfect itself as a community of persons.* . . .

The love between husband and wife and, in a derivative and broader way, the love between members of the same family — between parents and children, brothers and sisters and relatives and members of the household — is given life and sustenance by an unceasing inner dynamism leading the

family to ever deeper and more intense *communion*, which is
the foundation and soul of the *community* of marriage and the
family.

The first communion is the one which is established and
which develops between husband and wife: by virtue of the
covenant of married life, the man and woman "are no longer
two but one flesh" (Mt 19:6; Gn 2:24) and they are called to
grow continually in their communion through day-to-day
fidelity to their marriage promise of total mutual self-giving.

This conjugal communion sinks its roots in the natural comp-
lementarity that exists between man and woman, and is
nurtured through the willingness of the spouses to share their
entire life-project, what they have and what they are: for this
reason such communion is the fruit and the sign of a profoundly human need.

But in the Lord Christ, God takes up this human need,
confirms it, purifies it and elevates it, leading it to perfection
through the sacrament of Matrimony: the Holy Spirit, who is
poured out in the sacramental celebration, offers Christian
couples the gift of a new communion of love that is the living
and real image of that unique unity which makes of the
Church the indivisible Mystical Body of the Lord Jesus (nn.
18-19).

The Conjugal Union

The very word "conjugal" comes from the Latin word
conjux, meaning spouse, or from the Latin word *conjungere*,
meaning to join together. This concept, as Pope John Paul II has
pointed out, is fundamental to any understanding of Christian
marriage, in which a man and woman are joined together in
Christ. And since the primary relationship in marriage is that

between husband and wife, the document *Gaudium et Spes* states that "marriage is not merely for the procreation of children: its nature as an indissoluble compact between two people and the good of the children demand that the mutual love of the partners be properly shown, that it should grow and mature. Even in cases where, despite the intense desire of the spouses, there are no children, marriage still retains its character of being a whole manner and communion of life and preserves its value and indissolubility" (n. 50).

The conjugal union between husband and wife exists prior to the family and it will remain after the children have grown up and left home. In fact, Pope John Paul II has stated that the very first effect of marriage is "the Christian conjugal bond. . . . Conjugal love involves a totality in which all the elements of the person enter. . . . It aims at a deeply personal unity, the unity that, beyond union in one flesh, leads to forming one heart and soul; it demands indissolubility and faithfulness; and it is open to fertility. In a word, it is a question of the normal characteristics of all natural conjugal love, but with a new significance which not only purifies and strengthens them, but raises them to the extent of making them the expression of specifically Christian values" (*Familiaris Consortio*, n. 13).

Hence, the man and woman who enter upon the permanently shared life of marriage must be fortified by an authentic friendship-love if the marital contract is to be observed with all fidelity. Any self-seeking on the part of either spouse is diametrically opposed to the permanence and union of marriage. They are no longer two individuals seeking their own ends, but they are one in Christ. It follows, therefore, that entrance into married life requires a certain degree of maturity, and for that reason the Church has always insisted on proper preparation for this vocation, which is at once natural and sacramental. It is detrimental to the Church and to society at large to permit the marriage of two persons simply on the basis that there are no impediments to the marriage contract. Rather, in order to make the lifelong commitment that is required in the married state, there must be not only a generous mutual love, but also an understanding of the responsibilities and duties of married life and the recognition that this is a permanent union that can be dissolved only by the death of one of the spouses. They make their commitment "until death do us part."

Since marriage calls into play the various types of human love — physical, emotional and volitional — as well as the spiritual love which is charity, they must all be taken into account and properly coordinated. Normally we begin with a consideration of physical love, which constitutes the attraction of a man and woman for each other. This should not be the sole basis for deciding on marriage, but usually it will be a predomin-ant factor. Unless the man and woman experience some attraction for each other, it is hardly likely that their association will terminate in marriage. On the other hand, there is always the possibility that the mutual attraction is nothing more than a stimulation of lust, so that the person loved in this way is seen only as an object of sensate pleasure. In this context C.V. Heris has observed:

> Now it is certainly lawful to see marriage as a remedy for concupiscence, but marriage is a great deal more than the gratification of an animal instinct. It is the union of two persons, and each person must be loved for himself or herself. . . .
>
> What is more, marriage is not simply the union of two persons occupied exclusively in a selfish search for pleasure and forming a society closed upon itself. Marriage is destined for the procreation and education of the child. . . . If they want to give their carnal love all its meaning, they must direct it positively to this task of transmitting life, which is its basic purpose (*Spirituality of Love*, p. 188).

Physical love in marriage is normally accompanied by emotional love which is, as it were, the bridge between physical love and the higher love of friendship or volitional love. In women, the emotion of love usually plays a predominant role, and since the emotions are stimulated by sensate objects, a wife will seek to be affirmed in love by means of the kiss, the embrace, the loving glance and the tender touch. For that reason it is important that the husband exercise great tact and delicacy in order to respect the woman's innate sense of modesty and shame.

It is likewise on the emotional level that husbands and wives often find it difficult to understand and accept each other. Occupied as she is with the details of the household, the wife frequently becomes absorbed in or upset by what appears to the husband to be trivial matters. Moreover, there is such a difference between feminine and masculine psychology that the husband will often prefer the company of other men who share the same masculine interests, while the wife will gravitate toward her female friends, with whom she can chat about things of interest to women. Add to this the fact that after a short time in marriage both the husband and the wife cease to relate to each other in the same way as they did during their courtship. Something similar happens in every vocation, however; the monotony of everyday activities and duties sooner or later replaces the eagerness and fervor of emotional love. At the same time, this demonstrates that the love that brings joy, peace and harmony to the conjugal union must be something higher than purely physical love or even emotional love.

When properly controlled, physical and emotional love can serve as the springboard to an authentically human love between two persons who are united in friendship. On their wedding day the bride and groom dedicate their lives to each other, but it may be only after some years and consistent effort that they effectively realize this ideal of mutual self-giving. Some spouses, we must admit, never do reach it. They live their lives on the level of physical and emotional love, content to remain faithful to each other without ever really establishing the rapport of friendship. Yet the goal can be reached, because Christ has raised this natural contract of marriage to the level of a sacrament which transmits grace and charity to properly disposed spouses. Let us recall the admonition that was formerly given to the bride and groom at the time of their marriage:

> Because God himself is its author, marriage is of its nature a holy institution, requiring of those who enter it a complete and unreserved giving of self. But Christ our Lord added to the holiness of marriage an even deeper meaning and a higher beauty. He referred to marital love to describe his own love for his Church. . . . And so he gave to Christians a new vision of what married life ought to be — a life of self-sacrificing love like his own. . . . And whatever sacrifices you may hereafter have to make to preserve this common life, always make them generously. Sacrifice is usually difficult and irksome. Only love can make it easy; and perfect love can make it a joy.

We have already seen that the vehicle for the virtue of charity is friendship-love. Yet, since grace works through nature, or better, through the human personality, the love that is charity is perfectly compatible with physical and emotional love in marriage; consequently, it does not exclude the manifestations and enjoyment of love on those lower levels. What charity demands is that neither husband nor wife should selfishly seek in marriage their own personal satisfaction or benefit. This minimal self-denial suffices to elevate and purify the desires and gratifications of physical and emotional love.

Because of the physical and psychological differences between men and women, the functions of a husband and wife or a father and mother are not identical nor, in some cases, are they interchangeable. Each one has his or her distinct role to fulfill in marriage and family. Pope John Paul II touched on this point in *Familiaris Consortio*:

> Above all it is important to underline the equal dignity and responsibility of women with men. . . . There is no doubt that the equal dignity and responsibility of men and women fully justified women's access to public functions. On the other hand the true advancement of women requires that clear recognition be given to the value of their maternal and family role. . . . While it must be recognized that women have the same right as men to perform various public functions, society must be structured in such a way that wives and mothers are not in practice compelled to work outside the home, and that their families can live and prosper in a dignified way even when they themselves devote their full time to their own family (nn. 22-23, *passim*).

Sex in Marriage

The use and enjoyment of sex in marriage can pose a special challenge to the gift-love that is charity, since one or other of the spouses may seek only his or her self-gratification. On the other hand, if one's sexual education has consisted largely in prohibitions against sexual pleasure, then even after marriage a spouse may have feelings of guilt in performing the sex act. Paul Ricoeur has observed: "The idea of sacredness as separateness and untouchability has outlived the idea of sacredness as participation, but it tends to burden sexuality with a diffused sense of guilt" (cf. *Cross Currents*, Vol. XIV, p. 133). Once again, we turn to St. Paul for a theological explanation of this area of married life:

A man is better off having no relations with a woman. But to avoid immorality, every man should have his own wife and every woman her own husband. The husband should fulfill his conjugal obligations toward his wife, the wife hers toward her husband. A wife does not belong to herself but to her husband; equally, a husband does not belong to himself but to his wife. Do not deprive one another, unless perhaps by mutual consent for a time. . . . Then return to one another, that Satan may not tempt you through your lack of self-control (1 Cor 7:1-5).

As we have already seen, sexuality can operate on three different levels in the human person: the purely physical, which is genital sexuality; the emotional, which we call psychic sexuality; and the rational, which is genetic sexuality. It is on the third level that we find the love of friendship that should be the bond uniting the spouses and also the desire for parenthood. While St. Paul and Catholic tradition admit that the relief of concupiscence is a valid reason for performing the sex act in marriage, by its very nature the act has procreation as its purpose. Pope John Paul II has explained the role of sex in marriage in his Apostolic Exhortation:

Sexuality, by means of which man and woman give themselves to one another through the acts which are proper and exclusive to spouses, is by no means something purely biological, but concerns the innermost being of the human person as such. It is realized in a truly human way only if it is an integral part of the love by which a man and a woman commit themselves totally to one another until death. The total physical self-giving would be a lie if it were not the sign and fruit of a total personal self-giving, in which the whole person, including the temporal dimension, is present: if the person were to withhold something or reserve the possibility of deciding otherwise in the future, by this very fact he or she would not be giving totally.

This totality which is required by conjugal love also corresponds to the demands of responsible fertility. This fertility is directed to the generation of a human being, and so by its nature it surpasses the purely biological order and involves a whole series of personal values. For the harmonious growth of these values a persevering and unified contribution by both parents is necessary (*Familiaris Consortio*, n. 11).

When sexuality is treated as nothing more than an instinctual bodily need, it is reduced to a subhuman level; on the other hand, to overemphasize the ethical value of total sexual abstinence places Christian spouses in a moral dilemma. That is why it is important that parents, teachers and preachers should recognize that sexuality in marriage is both an expression of mutual conjugal love and a means of procreation. Any use or enjoyment of sex that increases and promotes the union of friendship love between the spouses is morally good; any use and enjoyment of sex that would militate against mutual love or close off the avenue to responsible fertility would be morally wrong. Married persons have no more right than the unmarried to use sexuality exclusively for selfish pleasure.

We can conclude from the foregoing that genital sexuality does have a value of its own in marriage, apart from its natural purpose of procreation. Otherwise it would be impossible to justify marital relations between a husband and wife when the wife has already conceived, when she is in her sterile period, or when she has passed the age of child-bearing. Considered in its exclusively physical reality, any natural bodily need or instinct is morally good, or at least morally indifferent. Consequently, we cannot attach sin to the physical act of sex *as such*, any more than we can say that all pleasurable eating is sinful. If it is morally good to place an act, it is also morally good to enjoy the pleasure that accompanies the act (cf. *Summa Theologiae*, Suppl., 49, 5).

If, therefore, there is any sinfulness attached to the enjoyment of genital sexuality, it will have to come from something extrinsic to the physical act itself. It will have to come from the person performing the act, as does all subjective morality. Thus, genital sexuality enjoyed by a person who is not married, or with someone other than one's spouse, is always seriously sinful. Moreover, sin may be involved in the *manner of performing the sexual act* (e.g., obtaining sexual pleasure in an unnatural way) or in the *motive for performing the sex act* (e.g., seeking one's own pleasure exclusively without any regard for the spouse). In other words, it is morally wrong to obstruct the physical act of sex from its purpose or to perform the act in a manner never intended by nature. As a matter of fact, mutual love in marriage is sometimes better preserved and fostered by non-genital manifestations of love; we do marriage a great disservice if we exaggerate the role of genital sexuality.

Parental Love

In his excellent commentary on *Familiaris Consortio*, Paul Conner states that the section that treats of God's plan for marriage and for the family is "the core of the apostolic message" (*Married in Friendship*, p. 11, a very helpful guide for teachers and counselors). And so it is, since it is there, as Pope John Paul II explains, that the covenant of conjugal love demands a totality of self-giving that "corresponds to the demands of responsible fertility" (n. 11). He then states that "conjugal love, while leading the spouses to the reciprocal 'knowledge' which makes them 'one flesh,' does not end with the couple, because it makes them capable of the greatest possible gift, the gift by which they become cooperators with God for giving life to a new human person. Thus the couple, while giving themselves to one another, give not just themselves but also the reality of children, who are a living reflection of their love, a permanent sign of conjugal unity and a living and inseparable synthesis of their being a father and a mother" (*Familiaris Consortio*, n. 14).

"These three, father, mother and child," says Walter Farrell, "are rightly spoken of as a human trinity; the child is a human holy spirit, the living love of those from whom it proceeds" (*Companion to the Summa*, Vol. 4, p. 408). This underlines the fact that marriage is not a private affair between a man and a woman; there must be not only a mutual friendship-love between husband and wife but their love should be creative. With the birth of the child, their love takes on a different quality and is, as it were, transformed from conjugal love to parental love. This means that their love extends beyond themselves, for which reason we have insisted that marriage must never be seen as a private affair between a man and a woman. In the words of C.V. Heris:

> Husband and wife must love each other in something greater than themselves, but this something has to be present for them to fall in love with it. It is found in the child, who is the fruit of their fertility, in this fragile and precious life which blossoms and grows like a flower toward a development which is at once human and divine. This life claims their tireless solicitude and, enlisting their love in its service, they turn their eyes away from themselves and are attached to the child. Their hands, which clasped each other on the day of marriage, have now loosened their grasp to take the child and lead him to his destiny (*Spirituality of Love*, p. 207).

This teaching, unfortunately, runs counter to contemporary culture in many parts of the world. Thanks to investigators who have promulgated techniques for greater pleasure in genital sexuality and those concerned with world population growth, who have instilled a sense of panic in the minds of many, there is a prevailing anti-life sentiment that threatens the well-being of many nations. The situation has become so paradoxical that the so-called "rights" of animals are placed above the rights of the human being. Witness, for example, the vast sums of money spent to publicize the plight of whales or an endangered animal species; yet scarcely a word is said about the thousands of children who die of malnutrition each year in some of the African countries. Numerous groups have been formed to promote the well-being of animals while civil law legalizes the right of a mother to murder her unborn child. Pope John Paul II has made a strong statement against this trend (as did Pope Paul VI in *Humanae Vitae*):

> The Church is called upon to manifest anew to everyone, with clear and stronger conviction, her will to promote human life by every means and to defend it against all attacks, in whatever condition or state of development it is found.

> Thus the Church condemns as a grave offense against human dignity and justice all those activities of governments or other public authorities which attempt to limit in any way the freedom of couples in deciding about children. Consequently any violence applied by such authorities in favor of contraception or, still worse, of sterilization and procured abortion, must be altogether condemned and forcefully rejected. Likewise to be denounced as gravely unjust are cases where, in international relations, economic help given for the advancement of peoples is made conditional on programs of contraception, sterilization and procured abortion.

> The Church is certainly aware of the many complex problems which couples in many countries face today in their task of transmitting life in a responsible way. She also recognizes the serious problem of population growth in the form it has taken in many parts of the world and its moral implications.

However, she holds that consideration in depth of all the
aspects of these problems offers a new and stronger confirma-
tion of the importance of the authentic teaching on birth
regulation re-proposed in the Second Vatican Council and in
the Encyclical *Humanae Vitae.*

For this reason, together with the Synod Fathers, I feel it is my
duty to extend a pressing invitation to theologians, asking
them to unite their efforts in order to collaborate with the
hierarchical Magisterium and to commit themselves to the
task of illustrating ever more clearly the biblical foundations,
the ethical grounds and the personalistic reasons behind this
doctrine (*Familiaris Consortio*, nn. 30-31).

Marriage is thus seen as the union of love in the service of
life. Sexuality is by its nature generative and creative. This is not
to deny, we repeat, that the conjugal act has other purposes
which are also morally good and legitimate. However, "any
denial of the fundamentally generative character of the sex act is
logically going to lead to conclusions which no Catholic moralist
is likely to admit; for once we assent to the proposition that there
can be legitimate sexual activity which is not by its nature
generative, there is little or no ground for condemning homosexual practices, mutual masturbation or other sexual aberrations"
(P. Starrs, "The Ends of Marriage," *Season*, Vol. 3, pp. 13 ff.).

Catholic teaching has always allowed for the limitation of
the family as long as the sexual act itself remains open to
procreation. This means that the only lawful method of restrict-
ing the number of children is by periodic abstinence, or what has
come to be known as natural family planning. What this means
is that the spouses may perform the sex act during the wife's
sterile period and refrain from sex during the few days each
month when she is fertile and therefore can conceive. No
doubt some persons find it difficult to understand why the
Church forbids artificial contraception but permits sex during

the wife's sterile period. Pope Paul VI answered this question in *Humanae Vitae*:

> If therefore there are reasonable grounds for spacing births, arising from the physical or psychological condition of husband or wife, or from external circumstances, the Church teaches that then married people may take advantage of the natural cycles immanent in the reproductive system and use their marriage at precisely those times that are infertile, and in this way control birth, a way which does not in the least offend the moral principles which we have just explained.

> Neither the Church nor her doctrine is inconsistent when she considers it lawful for married people to take advantage of the infertile period but condemns as always unlawful the use of means which directly exclude conception, even when the reasons given for the latter practice are neither trivial nor immoral. In reality these two cases are completely different. In the former, married couples rightly use a facility provided them by nature. In the latter, they obstruct the natural development of the generative process. It cannot be denied that in each case married couples, for acceptable reasons, are both perfectly clear in their intention to avoid children and mean to make sure that none will be born. But it is equally true that it is exclusively in the former case that husband and wife are ready to abstain from intercourse during the fertile period as often as for reasonable motives the birth of another child is not desirable. And when the infertile period recurs, they use their married intimacy to express their mutual love and safeguard their fidelity towards one another. In doing this they certainly give proof of a true and authentic love (n. 16).

The Sacrament of Matrimony

In listing the seven sacraments instituted by Christ, we normally speak of marriage as the sacrament of matrimony. The very word "matrimony" has an interesting and beautiful etymology. The dictionary tells us that the root of the word is from the Latin word *mater*, meaning mother. Hence matrimony primarily refers to motherhood. The father may be the head of the family, but the mother is the heart, and as such is the single most important influence on the life of the child. Moreover, the very word "matrimony" (motherhood) indicates that the natural purpose of the conjugal union is procreation.

Pope John Paul II has stated that:

> By virtue of the sacramentality of their marriage, spouses are bound to one another in the most profoundly indissoluble manner. Their belonging to each other is the real representation, by means of the sacramental sign, of the very relationship of Christ with the Church. . . . According to the plan of God, marriage is the foundation of the wider community of the family, since the very institution of marriage and conjugal love is ordained to the procreation and education of children, in whom they find their crowning. . . . Thus the couple, while giving themselves to one another, give not just themselves but also the reality of children, who are a living reflection of their love, a permanent sign of conjugal unity and a living and inseparable synthesis of their being a father and a mother (*Familiaris Consortio*, nn. 13-14).

The sacrament of matrimony is one of the social sacraments, the other one being the sacrament of holy orders. Like all the sacraments, it was instituted by Christ and confers its own special grace on those who receive it. It is unique in the sense that it is the bride and groom who administer the sacrament on each other; the priest witnesses the marriage and blesses it, but he does not administer the sacrament. By reason of their gift of mutual love and their promise of fidelity the bride and groom are capable of receiving through this sacrament all the graces they need to be faithful to their marriage vows and eventually to become Christian parents.

It is no surprise, therefore, that St. Paul compares the union of husband and wife to the union of Christ with his Church (cf. Ep 5:22-32). As Christ loved the Church to such an extent that he gave his life for the Church, so also the husband and wife are called upon to love one another with the totality of their being, sacrificing their own selfish interests for the good of the other.

There are, therefore, two kinds of love that should characterize Christian matrimony: spousal love and parental love. When their love is generous and mutual, the spouses are able to affirm each other in love and can complement and fulfill each other through their respective offices as husband and as wife. (For a detailed treatment of this aspect of married life, we highly recommend *Married in Friendship* by Paul Conner, pp. 121-166). Then, when they put their mutual love in the service of life and become parents, "they receive from God the gift of a new responsibility. Their parental love is called to become for the children the visible sign of the very love of God, 'from whom every family in heaven and on earth is named' (Ep 3:15)" (*Familiaris Consortio*, n. 14).

In the Book of Proverbs we find a beautiful tribute to motherhood, from which we derive the word "matrimony":

When one finds a worthy wife, her value is far beyond pearls. Her husband, entrusting his heart to her, has an unfailing prize. She brings him good, and not evil, all the days of her life. She is clothed with strength and dignity, and she laughs at the days to come. She opens her mouth in wisdom, and on her tongue is kindly counsel. She watches the conduct of her household, and eats not her food in idleness. Her children rise up and praise her; her husband, too, extols her: "Many are the women of proven worth, but you have excelled them all" (Pr 31:10-12, 25-29).

4

CELIBATE LOVE

When we hear the words "celibate" and "celibacy" we are likely to think immediately of Roman Catholic priests or of those Catholics who live the consecrated life, whether as religious or as members of a secular institute. The diocesan priest in the Latin rite is obliged to lead a celibate life, and this regulation dates as far back as the Council of Elvira in 306. It was repeated by the Council of Orange in 441 and the Council of Arles in 524, but by the end of the ninth century there was such a scandalous failure to observe celibacy that many persons in influential positions began to cite these abuses as reasons for abolishing the law of celibacy. They correctly stated that there is no necessary connection between celibacy and the priesthood, and they defended their position with references to Scripture and Tradition. They did not prevail, however, because St. Peter Damian (1072) and Pope Gregory VII (1085) were successful in defending and restating the discipline of celibacy for the Latin Church. The First Council of the Lateran (1123) declared major orders to be a diriment impediment to marriage, thus invalidating all attempted marriages by those in holy orders.

Nevertheless, periodically in the history of the Church, and especially at the time of an Ecumenical Council, the question of a married clergy was inevitably raised and debated. The strongest attack against a celibate clergy came from the Protestants, especially in the person of Martin Luther, who maintained that the promise of celibacy is null and void. The Council of Trent condemned Luther's assertions and repeated that holy orders constitutes a diriment impediment to marriage. This same law is in effect today and is stated in the *Code of Canon Law*, canon 1087, promulgated in 1983. However, it bears repeating that there is no necessary connection between celibacy and holy orders. It is the Church's law — and therefore human law — that demands celibacy of those in holy orders; consequently, the Church could just as readily allow for the ordination of married men. It has already taken half a step toward a married clergy by establishing the permanent diaconate, which can be received by married men (cf. canon 1031). Although some of the Fathers of the Eastern Churches considered celibacy to be the desirable norm for men in holy orders, it was never adopted universally. The Council *In Trullo*, held in 692, promulgated the following regulations for diocesan priests: (1) all bishops were obliged to practice continence, and if a married man were chosen or elected to be bishop, he had to leave his wife and she could retire to a convent; (2) priests, deacons and subdeacons were forbidden to marry after ordination, and if they were already married, they had to abstain from marital relations before celebrating the liturgy. Among the Greeks there was a preference that the parish priest should be a married man.

Pope John Paul II promulgated the first common *Code of Canon Law* for all the Oriental Churches on October 18, 1990. The new *Code* went into effect on October 1, 1991, and it legislates for the 21 Churches of the Eastern Rite which are grouped under five Mother Churches: Alexandrian, Antiochian, Byzantine, Armenian and Chaldean. The legislation concerning those in holy orders can be summarized as follows: (1) only a baptized male can be admitted to holy orders (canon 754); (2) once ordained, he may not attempt marriage, even civilly (canon 762); (3) the Church does, however, recognize and approve of both a celibate clergy and a married clergy according to the law of the particular church or the Holy See (canon 758); (4) bishops may not be married (can. 180), and before a married man can be ordained, he needs permission from his wife in writing (canon 769); (5) those who wish to be permanent deacons may be ordained after three years of study, but ordination to the priest-hood must be preceded by four years of study (canons 354 and 760).

So much for the question of celibacy for men in holy orders. The second group of celibates covered by the legislation of the Church are members of institutes of the consecrated life. The revised *Code of Canon Law* describes this state of life:

Life consecrated through profession of the evangelical counsels is a stable form of living, in which the faithful follow Christ more closely under the action of the Holy Spirit, and are totally dedicated to God, who is supremely loved. By a new and special title they are dedicated to seek the perfection of charity in the service of God's Kingdom, for the honor of God, the building up of the Church, and the salvation of the world. They are a splendid sign in the Church, as they foretell the heavenly glory.

Christ's faithful freely assume this manner of life in institutes of consecrated life, which are canonically established by the competent ecclesiastical authority. By vows or by other sacred bonds, in accordance with the laws of their own institutes, they profess the evangelical counsels of chastity, poverty and obedience. Because of the charity to which these counsels lead, they are linked in a special way to the Church and its mystery (canon 573).

There are two general types of consecrated life treated in the *Code of Canon Law*: the religious life, whose members are required to live in community (canon 607); and the secular institutes, whose members should be predominantly lay Christians dedicated to the sanctification of the temporal order (canon 710). A third distinct classification pertains to members of societies of the apostolic life, which "resemble institutes of consecrated life. . . . Living a fraternal life in common in their own special manner, they strive for the perfection of charity through the observance of the constitutions. Among these societies are some in which the members, through a bond defined in the constitutions, undertake to live the evangelical counsels" (Canon 731). [Readers who are interested in a detailed treatment of consecrated life will find it in the recently published book, *Christian Totality*, by B. Cole and P. Conner, St. Paul Publications, Bandra, Bombay 400 050, India, 1990.]

In addition to priests of the Latin rite and men and women in the consecrated life, there is yet another group of people who are obliged to live a celibate life, namely, all those Christians who are as yet unmarried or for one reason or another do not intend to marry. Since all the rights and privileges of marriage are restricted to lawfully wedded spouses, unmarried persons are forbidden to indulge in sexual pleasure, regardless of the manner in which that pleasure is obtained. They are bound to observe chastity just as strictly as those who are committed to a chaste life by reason of a vow (members of the consecrated life) or the legislation of the Church (unmarried deacons and priests of the Roman Catholic Church).

With very few exceptions, most of the literature on the spirituality of the laity has been oriented to the married state or to persons in lay institutes of the consecrated life. The numerous lay Christians living an unmarried life in the world are often overlooked, in spite of the fact that in modern times their number is increasing. Consequently, it is important to note that what we shall say about celibate love and friendship will apply to all three groups, although there are obvious differences in the condition and state of life of each group.

The Meaning of Celibacy

At the very outset we want to emphasize the fact that although a celibate must forego the rights and duties of marriage, he or she must never renounce the ability to love. The celibate heart must never be a selfish, sterile heart, because, as St. Augustine reminds us, our hearts were made for love.

The word "celibate" means an unmarried person: one who is as yet not married but will eventually marry, or one who has voluntarily renounced marriage and the possibility of a spouse and family. In both cases, the individual is obliged to refrain from all voluntary sexual pleasure because that, as we have seen, is restricted to spouses in marriage. There is, of course, a difference between "temporary" celibacy and the permanent, voluntary choice of a celibate life. In the first case a young man or woman will eventually meet and fall in love with his or her future spouse. In the beginning of their courtship their love will be experienced to a great extent on the sensate and emotional level. Consequently, there will be manifestations and expressions of love on those levels, and that is perfectly natural and good as long as the expressions of their love are in accordance with Christian moral teaching.

But those who voluntarily choose the celibate life will be required not only to renounce marriage and the use and enjoyment of genital sex; they must also abstain from those expressions of sensate and emotional love that are proper to courtship and marriage. In an age of exaggerated sexual freedom celibates need to be especially careful not to become involved in a sensate or purely emotional relationship. If they do, they may well lose the very freedom that the celibate life offers. They must, there-fore, not only be chaste but they must be *continent*. When treating of the evangelical counsels that are the essential ele-ments of the consecrated life, St. Thomas Aquinas speaks of continence rather than chastity, and what he says about conti-nence applies to all who are not married:

> The religious state requires the removal of those things which impede a man from giving himself entirely to God's service. But the use of carnal union withdraws the soul from being entirely devoted to the service of God, and for two reasons. First, because of the intensity of the pleasure, the frequent experience of which, says Aristotle, increases concupiscence. That is why the use of sexual pleasure withdraws the soul from that perfect intention of tending to God. . . . Secondly, because of the preoccupation it causes a man in governing his wife and children and the temporal goods needed for their support. . . . Therefore perpetual continence is required for religious perfection, as is voluntary poverty (*Summa Theologiae*, II-II, 186, 4).

There is a problem, however, as regards the teaching of St. Thomas Aquinas and also as regards the teaching of St. Paul, who states that "the unmarried man is busy with the Lord's affairs, concerned with pleasing the Lord, but the married man is busy with this world's demands and occupied with pleasing his wife. This means he is divided. The virgin — indeed, any unmarried woman — is concerned with things of the Lord, in pursuit of holiness in body and spirit. The married woman, on the other hand, has the cares of this world to absorb her and is concerned with pleasing her husband. I am going into this for your own good. I have no desire to place restrictions on you, but I do want to promote what is good, what will help you to devote yourselves entirely to the Lord" (1 Cor 7:32-35).

The problem is that both St. Thomas Aquinas and St. Paul

seem to be saying that the choice of a celibate life is always for the purpose of being consecrated to the Lord or the service of the Lord. It is true, of course, that many celibates are priests or members of institutes of the consecrated life and hence devote themselves entirely or at least primarily to the service of the Lord. But what about a lay person who remains unmarried for other than religious reasons and does not make a formal commitment to celibacy? A woman may forego marriage in order to devote herself to the care of her aged parents; a man may feel that his military career, diplomatic service or professional duties are incompatible with marriage and raising a family. In neither instance can it be said that they are living a "consecrated" celibacy.

Moreover, the teaching of St. Paul concerning married people seems to curtail greatly the possibility of their dedication to the service of the Lord. It seems as if St. Paul is reluctant to approve of marriage as a state of life for Christians; marriage then becomes a solution for those who cannot practice continence. Some persons may have a similar problem with the fact that Christ reprimanded the motherly Martha and said that the contemplative Mary had chosen "the better part" (Lk 10:38-42). To complicate the problem, we note that in our day the Church allows married men to become permanent deacons, thus admitting them to holy orders and making them members of the clergy. This, in turn, perpetuates the discussion concerning the possibility of married priests for the Latin Church; it also calls for a re-evaluation of the significance of celibacy in the Christian life. C.V. Heris has discussed this question at some length:

> No doubt, in [St. Paul's] opinion — and it has been the opinion of the Church throughout the centuries — virginity is better than marriage. But the reasons for this preference must be examined. . . .

St. Paul does not place the excellence of virginity in the simple abstention from carnal intercourse, as if intercourse represented something shameful and blameworthy. Whether one remains a virgin or marries, both things are good in themselves. Moreover, if a person is tempted to sins of the flesh outside marriage and feels he is not strong enough to overcome his passions, it is better for him to marry. . . .

What makes virginity superior to marriage in itself is thus not the simple fact of renouncing the pleasures of the flesh permitted by conjugal union. The superiority comes from something else: the advantage that virginity affords and the end to which it is ordered. The advantages or goods of virginity are the absence of worldly preoccupation such as marriage knows, the liberty of soul which makes it easy to practice prayer, the holiness it brings to soul and body. . . . Exemption from the trials and complications of family life is good only in the measure that it permits the soul to free itself more easily from temporal things in order to apply itself to spiritual realities and tend more readily to perfection. . . . This is really the justification of virginity, and the reason why it is better than marriage. It chooses more apt means to detach the soul from the world and to unite it to God (*Spirituality of Love*, pp. 210-211).

It would seem to follow from the foregoing that the only justification for the celibate life is consecration to the service of God. But what of those persons who choose the celibate life in order to devote themselves to some human endeavor such as works of charity, professional duties, social work, study and research, or the arts? This question was investigated by theologians such as Karl Rahner, Hans Urs von Balthasar and Jean Beyer. Although they did not agree with each other on every point concerning the relationship between permanent celibacy and the consecrated life, we can offer a few conclusions as a result of their studies. First, permanent celibacy does not of itself constitute a consecration to the service of the Lord; therefore, it does not necessarily place one in the state of the consecrated life. Secondly, those who do embrace the consecrated life will do so either as hermits, consecrated virgins, religious, or members of a secular institute. The societies of apostolic life, as we have noted above, are not classified under the title of consecrated life, although the members who make a vow or promise of continence in those societies would surely live a consecrated celibacy.

We may note in passing that since the members of many religious institutes of the active life no longer obey the legislation of the Church concerning some of the essential elements of their manner of life, it would seem that the Church should state officially that they no longer have the right to be classified as religious. It would be more in keeping with reality to classify them legally as members of a secular institute or a society of apostolic life. And even if the Church does not make an official declaration to that effect, one must in fact conclude that such institutes are no longer institutes of religious life.

A good deal of the confusion today concerning the consecrated life has arisen from the fact that there has been a definite change in the theology of the consecrated life. Traditionally, the distinguishing mark of persons consecrated to God was separation from the world, even to the point of living a completely cloistered life behind grilles and walls. But with the movement toward an active, apostolic life outside the cloister that began with new forms of religious life initiated by the canons regular and the mendicant friars, and came to its peak in the Society of Jesus, the essence of the consecrated life now consists in the evangelical counsels of poverty, chastity and obedience. And of these three counsels, the fundamental one is perpetual continence, since the other two counsels admit of great flexibility. For example, the observance of poverty in a cloistered, contemplative religious institute will differ greatly from that in an active, apostolic institute; obedience in the

Society of Jesus will differ from the practice of obedience among the Dominicans and the Franciscans. Yet the practice of perpetual continence — popularly known as the vow of chastity — will be the same for all. In the context of our discussion, therefore, we see two classes of Christ's faithful: those who enter the married state and those who remain celibate, whether as clergy, persons in the consecrated life, or individuals who for one reason or another have renounced marriage.

The chastity of continence, which is required of celibates, is more demanding than marital chastity. As its name indicates, it enables a person to exercise self-control or self-containment in response to the demands made by the sexual urge. Put another way, continence is the virtue or strength of character by which a person resists the lustful desire for sexual pleasure. However, the decision to lead a celibate life does not automatically control or restrain the demands of the sex instinct. Whether a person is continent or not, the sexual urge will normally follow its own cycle and at times may be experienced as a vehement sensate desire. Even some of the great saints and mystics, such as St. Catherine of Siena and St. Rose of Lima, were subjected to severe temptations in this area. But sin is not in any faculty, organ or instinct of the body; it is in the will. For that reason St. Thomas Aquinas states that continence is a matter of one's voluntary choice: "Whereas the continent, though they undergo strong movements of passion, effectively decide not to be led astray by them, the incontinent surrender to them, though their reason forbids. Consequently continence resides in the faculty of the soul that makes choices, and that is the will" (Summa Theologiae, II-II, 155, 3).

Just as some persons are not suited for married life, so also there are some who cannot live a celibate life. At first glance it may seem that since the sexual instinct has a *social* orientation, its natural purpose being procreation, any person can live the celibate life if he or she so chooses. Even in marriage there may be periods of time in which the spouses choose not to or cannot make use of sex. A permanent abstinence from sex should not change the situation essentially. Consequently, there can be no ill effects psychologically if an individual leads a continent life as a celibate. Dr. Alexis Carrel has made an interesting observation in this regard:

> Freud has rightly emphasized the capital importance of sexual impulses in the activities of consciousness. However, his observations refer chiefly to sick people. His conclusions should not be generalized to include normal individuals, especially those who are endowed with a strong nervous system and mastery over themselves. While the weak, the nervous and the unbalanced become more abnormal when their sexual appetites are repressed, the strong are rendered still stronger by practicing such a form of asceticism (*Man, the Unknown*, p. 144).

Consequently, St. Paul gave the following advice to the Corinthians: "To those not married and to widows I have this to say: It would be well if they remain as they are, even as I do myself; but if they cannot exercise self-control, they should marry. It is better to marry than to be on fire" (1 Cor 7:8-9).

But whether one marries or renounces marriage, Roger Schutz of Taizé has stated that "both Christian marriage and Christian celibacy are valid only in terms of an effort at obedience to the Lord of the Church. . . . Approached in any other spirit, they will quickly become merely a return to preoccupation with oneself in which we no longer love for the sake of Christ and the Gospel, and in which our love, far from giving of itself, will seek above all to possess and dominate everything for its own satisfaction. . . . If the love of Christ does not seize our being in its totality, if we do not allow ourselves to be enkindled by his love, we cannot aspire to the fullness of Christian marriage or of Christian celibacy" (*Living Today for God*, Helicon Press, 1962).

The person who chooses marriage and family will necessarily experience the preoccupation and anxiety that accompany the care of a spouse and children. Conversely, the person who chooses the celibate life will necessarily experience at times a certain loneliness and lack of fulfillment. The saintly Archbishop Martinez of Mexico City has made a beautiful statement concerning celibacy and the sublimation of the genetic or parental instinct. If celibates would apply it to their lives, they would not blame the loneliness of celibacy for the crisis in morale that is experienced by some priests and religious:

> Not a single one of the shades of love must be lacking to the soul for whom God is all. By consecrating oneself to him, one loses nothing and gains much. . . .

> There is one shade of love that our heart necessarily longs for: it is the reflection of the paternity of the Father. Virgin souls do not have to relinquish it. . . . It has Jesus as its end. The whole Christ is not only the one born of Mary, but the one born unceasingly in the Church, the one formed in all the elect. . . .

> No doubt the Holy Spirit forms Christ in us, but we cooperate in his formation in a similar, though a very remote manner, to the way Mary cooperated in the formation of Jesus in his real body. Jesus is consequently *our son mystically*. . . .

> If, after considering Jesus in myself, I consider him in others, the apostolic life takes on the exalted proportions of a paternity such as St. Paul conceived it. Considered in this way, how can flesh and blood and human designs be seen in the holy affection for souls, in the exquisite work of forming Christ in them? (*Spirituality of Archbishop Martinez*, Herder, St. Louis, 1966).

Consequently, we can hardly praise the celibate life simply as a renunciation of marriage and abstinence from sexual pleasure. Such a celibacy could be the result of a distorted view of human sexuality or chosen for purely selfish reasons. The celibate should not want to be free *from* something, but *for* something. St. Paul, St. Augustine and St. Thomas Aquinas, as we have seen, all insist that celibacy and virginity are praiseworthy because of their end and purpose, namely, freedom to be concerned about the things of God. Michel Quoist has written: "It's hard to love everyone and to claim no one. It's hard to shake a hand and not want to retain it. It's hard to be alone" (*Prayers*, p. 66). But there will always be an element of sacrifice in every state of life, whether it be marriage or celibacy. Both types of life call for a generous love that can rise above self-centered interests and can experience the joy of giving.

Celibate Love and Friendship

We repeat that although the celibate renounces the love of a particular person in marriage, he or she is not expected to reject all human love. The celibate heart should not be a cold and sterile heart. Yet there are certain types of love that are incompatible with the celibate state. The sexual urge and sexual energy remain, stronger in some than in others, but all who are unmarried are forbidden to indulge in any form of genital sexuality.

Fortunately, physical sexuality is not necessarily linked to love, since a husband and wife who no longer make use of the sex act are nevertheless still in love with each other. Moreover, physical love and the sexual urge can be sublimated to higher goals and more spiritual manifestations. The challenge is found on the level of emotional, sensate love. There is nothing to forbid the celibate, any more than the married person, from the controlled and reasonable expression and enjoyment of emotional love. But the celibate soon learns from experience that it is difficult to live that type of life unless he or she is in complete control of sensate satisfactions and the movements of emotional love. The reason for this is, as we have seen, that the emotions are basically self-centered; consequently, when emotional love predominates, there is a temptation to love the other person for oneself and even to descend to the lower level of purely physical gratification.

The celibate's love for another person may begin on the sensate or emotional level, as does that of a young man and woman who fall in love, but it must not remain there. Celibate love requires not only a life of total continence but also a high degree of control of emotional love. For that reason Bernard Haring maintains that "a self-centered adolescent is not capable of celibacy, even if he has no trouble with sex" ("Address to Major Superiors of Religious Men," 1965). Even in marriage, where physical and emotional love play an important role, the ideal of marital love is to become transformed into the generous love of authentic friendship.

Perhaps some celibates feel frustrated because in spite of living a chaste life they are still basically self-centered and possessive. They recognize that all manifestations of physical love and any enjoyment of genital sex are excluded from the celibate state. Nevertheless, if they have not risen above the sensate level in their lifestyle, they may very easily transfer the satisfaction of their sensate desires from genital sex to food or drink or some other form of self-gratification. Others there are who in their human relations are capable only of emotional attachments, which are bound to be selective and possessive. It is here that we encounter what has been called "particular friendship," which must be strictly curtailed in any form of community life, including the family. The reason for this is that such friendships tend to be exclusive and possessive, and both of these attitudes are diametrically opposed to the sharing and *esprit de corps* that should prevail in a community.

It is doubtless a delicate question when it comes to friendship among celibates, whether between the sexes or within the same sex. It goes without saying that if the emotion of love that is directed to another person stimulates a desire for possession of that person or even arouses the desire for sexual gratification, then the celibate can have nothing to do with that kind of love.

The signs of a "particular friendship" are readily discernible in any type of community. The persons involved will constantly seek each other's company and will spend long periods of time with each other, engaged in very private conversation. They may even come to the point of touching or caressing each other, as do a young man and woman in courtship. They will also jealously exclude all others who may want to enter the circle of that friendship. The passion of love, we repeat, is self-centered and possessive. That is why particular friendships tend to be exclusive, possessive and eventually obsessive.

Does it follow, then, that the celibate must severely repress all the emotions, including the emotion of love, by a strict asceticism? We can answer at once that it is not so much a question of repression as of self-control, of subjecting the emotions to the guidance of intellect and will. Any movement of strong love — even of friendship-love — will normally be accompanied by an emotional reaction. Empathy, tenderness and warmth of feeling are the natural concomitants of ardent love. The difference is that in an authentic friendship the movements of the emotion of love are under the guidance and control of reason and will.

In addition to that, the passions can be sublimated to serve higher ends, and this will happen when volitional love intervenes. As we have seen, volitional love is essentially a gift-love by which we seek primarily the good of the other instead of desiring the other for yourself, as happens when the emotion of love is the dominating power.

Authentic friendship requires that we renounce possessiveness and self-seeking, and if this cannot be done in a particular relationship, the only alternative is to end that relationship. The separation may be extremely painful, but it will be a liberating experience as well. The individual is then free to cultivate the love of friendship, which for the celibate must be closer to paternal or maternal love than to spousal love. Then, whether it be a question of friendship between two persons of the same sex or of the opposite sex, the friendship can be very fruitful and beneficial on both a human and a spiritual level. Two such friends can fully understand and experience the truth of the statement made by St. Thomas Aquinas: *"Caritas amicitia est"* (Charity is friendship).

As regards preparation for living a celibate life, the practice of the Church — gathering youngsters and adolescents to live together in preparation for the priesthood or religious life — has come under strong criticism from theologians and psychologists. They base their argument on the fact that since the natural vocation for men and women is marriage, the natural environment for youngsters is the home and family. Therefore, boys and girls should normally grow up together. One result of this criticism has been the closing of many "minor" seminaries and pre-novitiate formation centers. It continues to be the policy of the Church, however, that where necessary and expedient, minor seminaries are still to be encouraged.

In the past few decades there has been a swing in the opposite direction, affecting not only young seminarians and postulants for the religious life but also young people in general. Paul Conner, in his comprehensive study entitled *Celibate Love*, has made some very helpful observations concerning the present trend:

With regard to fulfilling love, two possible problems suggest themselves concerning the training of young men and women for living and working together in adult life. Imprudence in either direction invites danger. The first difficulty lies in the frequent assumption that if young people of both sexes are put together often enough they will develop the capacity for healthy, interpersonal relationships. This is psychologically untenable. A reasonable amount of wholesome contact is most helpful, but only on condition that in their training personal adequacy be stressed as an essential prerequisite for fulfilling love. If, individually, young men and women are taught to assume the responsibility for becoming adequate *as persons*, they will respect each other as such. They will have the strength of will as well as the warmth of feeling to honor this respect in their behavior. A reverent regard and appreciation for themselves and for each other as mature persons is the starting point for developing authentic, fulfilling relationships between men and women.

A second current assumption is equally without justification, namely, that as necessary preparation for genuine love relationships as adults, young men and women must become deeply, even erotically, involved with one another. Psychological studies of such involvements show that in fact a majority of these young people eventually become repulsive to each other. They may also experience deep-seated feelings of guilt that reduce their capability for genuine love relationships later on in life (pp. 35-36).

PSYCHOLOGY OF LOVE AND SEXUALITY

Conrad W. Baars, M.D. († 1981)

5

SEXUAL DIFFERENCES AND DEGREES OF LOVE

The world of today, at least the Western world, could be described without too much exaggeration as an unloving and sexualized world. The preoccupation with deviate sexual conduct in literature, the movies and television; the ready availability of pornographic materials in stores and through the mail; the lack of sexual restraint as a matter of course not only among college students but also among high-school students and even youngsters in the elementary grades; the frightening increase in juvenile delinquency and drug addiction which are often accompanied by sexual license — these are but a few of the reasons for branding our culture as a sexualized one. It seems reasonable to assume that the ubiquitous erotic stimulation to which our youngsters are exposed from their first year of life through television, comic books and videos, advertising and rock music has contributed significantly to an earlier sexual maturity of our children. It is estimated that youngsters today reach full physical development two or three years earlier than the youngsters of half a century ago. At the same time the age of emotional and

intellectual maturity is several years later than that of the adolescent fifty years ago. Perhaps this is due to the fact that our youth
are faced with a much greater number and variety of problems
which have to be resolved before they can attain emotional and
personal stability. The tremendous technological progress and
instant world-wide communication, the ever-increasing population, with less privacy and more togetherness, more years spent
in school in overcrowded classrooms and little personal contact
with professors and teachers, and the large number of "nuclear
families" separated from relatives because of job relocations —
these are some of the factors related to this delayed emotional
and intellectual maturity.

The result of all this has been an ever-widening gap between the age of puberty, in which the capacity to perform the
reproductive act is attained, and the age at which the adolescent
begins to be capable of performing the sexual act in a manner
proper to a human being — the age of sexual maturity in the
wider sense of the term. It is at this time that the young adult
should arrive at the psychic maturity of responsibility and freedom that makes it possible to give oneself totally to another
person.

It is not at all uncommon to place all the blame on the
younger generation for their sexual promiscuity, teen-age preg-
nancies, homosexual activity, and social delinquencies. The
"young people of today" are compared unfavorably with the
better and more mature "young people of yesterday." We all
know that the older generation is readily inclined to speak with
disdain of the modern ideas and behavior of the younger generation. However, we sometimes fail to realize that young people do
not always understand and appreciate the things of the past; at
the same time, they have not yet formed their own ideas and
standards. Save for exceptional cases, young people will absorb
and reflect the ideas of the older generation. They do that quite

readily and often without complete awareness, because their minds are open and receptive.

Hence, if young people have different ideas about dating, resent parental control, want unrestrained sexual freedom, or want free access to every and any book or movie, it is not so much because young people today are different, but because we adults are uncertain and in turmoil. And while it is true that young people are able to make fairly independent and responsible choices, the older generation has to present them with the kinds of conduct and attitudes from which they can choose. Therefore, since our sexualized culture is primarily a reflection of the confusion of adults concerning love and sexuality, we have the responsibility to resolve our confusion by a proper understanding of the meaning of human love and sexuality. Only then can we give young people the guidance that they need and desire so much.

Man and Woman

It is regrettable that the only English word to describe the differences between man and woman refers chiefly to the anatomical, physical differences. The Dutch language has the advantage that the word *seksualiteit* or "sexuality" refers to the physical differences between man and woman while the word *geslachtelykheid* may be used to indicate the sum total of both the psychic and the physical male or female characteristics. The latter Dutch word corresponds to the English word "gender," which seems to be used only in grammar. But it is important to differentiate between genital sexuality, which is sexuality in a very limited sense, and that which is designated by the terms "male sex" and "female sex," namely, everything that collectively distinguishes the male from the female.

Further evidence of this preoccupation with genital or

physical sexual differences to the exclusion of all other male and female characteristics can be seen in the changed meaning of the word "erotic." Originally it referred to Eros, the Greek god of love, but as currently defined in the dictionary, it is restricted to sexual love and desire, to the exclusion, one might say, of the essential characteristics of truly human love. [Editor's Note: The comments of Dr. Rollo May concerning erotic love are well worth repeating here.]

> Eros in our day is taken as a synonym for "eroticism" or sexual titillation. . . . One wonders whether everyone has forgotten the fact that Eros, according to no less an authority than St. Augustine, is the power which drives men toward God. . . . The end towards which sex points is gratification and relaxation; whereas Eros is a desiring, a longing, a forever reaching out, seeking to expand. . . . For Eros is the power that *attracts* us. The essence of Eros is that it draws us from ahead, whereas sex pushes us from behind. . . . Sex is a need, but Eros is a desire; and it is this admixture of desire which complicates love. . . . It can be agreed that the aim of the sex act in its zoological and physiological sense is indeed the orgasm. But the aim of Eros is not; Eros seeks union with the other person in delight and passion, and the procreating of new dimensions which broaden and deepen the being of both persons. . . . The French have a saying which . . . carries more truth: "The aim of desire is not its satisfaction but its prolongation" (*Love and Will*, pp. 72-75, *passim*).

Because it is too often ignored in textbooks of psychology and psychiatry, I think it is important to give a description of the natural, God-given, non-genital sexual characteristics of the adult man and woman. An understanding of these characteristics is necessary in order to apply correctly what we shall say later about the nature of human love. At least it will serve as a measure by which we can judge the effects of our love on other people.

Our love should fulfill ourselves and those we love; moreover, both we and they should be fulfilled not only as human beings but as men and women. The fully developed male and female characteristics are a necessary condition for human happiness on the natural level because they are necessary for love to be given and received. In addition to this, they are absolutely essential if supernatural grace is to become operative and fruitful in the lives of individuals.

Parents should therefore possess the well-developed male and female characteristics respectively if their children are to attain maturity and happiness as adult men and women. By the same token, the absence or distortion of the male and female characteristics — or for that matter, their exaggerated presence in a member of the opposite sex — is a reliable indicator that the faculty for loving may be seriously impaired. If this occurs in parents, the children may likely reflect this disorder in the form of emotional and mental disturbances.

This warning should be heeded particularly by those entrusted with the selection of candidates for the priesthood and religious life. In fact, the personalities of the parents and the atmosphere of love in the home are much more reliable criteria than those of the economic or professional status of the parents. Since many of the so-called "better families" are totally submerged in our contemporary culture, which is far from healthy, one may rightly question whether or not such families can produce children who are capable of becoming mature adults in any profession or state of life.

The manner in which a man or a woman experiences life and love, the burden of their work or profession, their contribution to marriage and family or, for that matter, to the celibate state, is distinctly different. And yet, in spite of these typical differences, accentuated as they are by heredity, temperament, race and environment, there is a basic equality between men and women; otherwise, how could they be attuned to each other? The woman, first of all, may be compared to a mountain lake which receives the waters that flow from the mountain peaks, purifies them and sends them downward as a mighty river. Woman's most profound characteristic is her motherliness, not necessarily that of motherhood, of giving life, but that of cherishing life in others so that it may grow and unfold in all its glory. As Gertrud von le Fort has said so beautifully in her book, *The Eternal Woman*: "Wherever woman is most profoundly herself, she is so, not as herself but as surrendered; and wherever she is surrendered, there she is also bride and mother."

Nature has given woman a special inner wholesomeness or, to put it in psychological terminology, the different faculties of her being are more integrated than those of a man. And since those faculties operate more intimately together, the woman tends to be involved in things more as a total being. This total involvement is, for instance, manifested in a woman's way of thinking, understanding and judging. Instead of performing these functions in the cold, analytical manner of a man, she does so in close association with her heart, her feelings. This gives her an intuitive and sympathetic understanding of the personal life of those who are close to her. As Pascal put it: "The heart has its reasons which reason does not know."

A woman's total involvement also manifests itself in her manner of loving. She devotes herself with her whole soul and all her strength to those she loves, but by the same token she is hurt much more deeply and completely when her love is not returned. While a man may lose his faith in others because of their evil deeds, the woman is often able to believe in them in spite of everything, hoping that the good in them will prevail over the evil. Once again, it is the close cooperation between head and heart which makes this possible, just as it enables her to bear up under suffering with amazing fortitude. The man often succumbs to impatience or despair when he suffers, but the woman's hopeful endurance often brings back his strength and courage.

The man's existential stance, his being-in-the-world, is very different, more complex, more divided. He must be a loving husband and father but he must also be dedicated to his work or profession and to the community. His head and heart, his intellect and emotions are less integrated than those of a woman. For that reason he thinks more clearly and logically, without interference from his emotions and feelings. This, of course, is very helpful for maintaining a competitive position in his work, but it may cause him to become aggressive and even violent when his passion is aroused. His love for his family and his desire to be with them alternate with the urge to leave them and dedicate himself to his work, his personal interests or the demands of public life. Then, once again, he is drawn to his home and family. The woman, on the other hand, has only one love — her husband, home and family — but the husband has the difficult task of maintaining the proper balance between his two loves: wife, home and family on the one hand, and work, personal interests and community obligations on the other. The man must be active, but without becoming so busily occupied that he loses his taste for inner quiet and contemplation. He must be aggressive and determined to persevere in his work; he must oppose the evils in the world without losing his respect for others. He must have control over his emotions, but without repressing them and thus destroying all empathy and tenderness. He must be willing and able, so to speak, to "lend" his powers of reason to his wife to help her bring order and harmony to her emotional life when she needs it.

All this and more has been beautifully described by Edith Stein (Blessed Teresa Benedicta), the Jewish German philosopher who became a Carmelite nun and died in the concentration camp at Auschwitz. I quote her description of the differences between man and woman, husband and wife, and particularly the manner in which these differences are viewed nowadays and used as a basis for superiority or unfair advantage by the opposite sex, when they should actually complement each other to the perfection of man and woman. Further, I quote Edith Stein because as a woman she was in a better position to understand what a woman really is or ought to be.

> Only a feminist, in the fever of the extreme, will deny that woman's calling differs from man's, that for all their common human nature, the souls of men and women have each their own design. The clear and irrefutable word of Scripture utters what from the very beginning of the world daily experience teaches: woman is made to be the helpmate of man and his mother. For this her body is fitted and this is the endowment of her soul, tending more toward people than toward things and affairs, more toward the concrete than toward the abstract, tending always toward the living, the personal, the whole. It is the whole she wishes to foster — not, for instance, the mind at the expense of the heart, nor mind and heart at the expense of the body.
>
> This same motherly bent toward wholeness marks woman's cognitive life. What speak to her first, and are her joy, are image and encounter, not concept and law, so that she does not go out after fixed and solid systems but rather opens herself to contents, wide, flowing and colorful. Her knowing, much like the artist's, is a waiting on and listening to truth rather than its pursuit. . . . To nurse and keep and shield and help grow — this is every woman's natural motherly desire and skill, and to them are joined her desire and skill as companion. Her gift and happiness are in sharing in another person's life, and sharing means to her, sharing in everything that concerns the person she loves, in the great things and the small, in his joys and sorrows, in his work and his problems.

A man is likely to be wrapt up in his affairs, and even more so in a cause, expecting from others interest and ready service; but more often than not, he finds it hard to bring them and their concerns into focus. For a woman, who is more nearly timeless, who is never so much a "contemporary" as a man, this adjustment is natural. With the ease and flexibility that are her talent, she can enter sympathetically into and understand fields otherwise remote from her, in which she would have no concern were it not for her interest in a person. And it is her overflowing wealth of heart, her almost limitless ability to devote herself, her patience, that help make her partake in man's life, a partaking which awakens his strength and multiplies his achievements. She does it with patience, for while man may be able to do more, she can endure more; while he has greater thrusting power, she has more energy in store. So important in man's life is this hidden care, this rearing and mothering, that the mature man still needs it — even he, and precisely he. Not for nothing does man call his beloved his "tender sweetheart."

Because man serves his cause more directly and woman more for his sake, it is appropriate that she do so under his guidance. Scripture's demand for her obedience to him as her head is not a caprice, is not against the logic of things. On the contrary, the biblical command gives word to the metaphysics of the sexes. If their partnership is seen under the image of a tree, man is the tuft, woman the root, the whole hidden root bearing even the highest tuft and the sunlit tuft bearing even the furthest root; the root filling the top with its strength, the top governing the root by its encompassing power.

As woman's talents are tied in her to a wounded nature, they are always in peril of being distorted. Her gift for the personal, if not guarded, may become preoccupation with herself and a desire for others' preoccupation with her; it may become vanity, an inordinate wish for praise, or an uncontrolled need for communication. On the other hand, it may turn into an excessive, indiscreet interest in others, into curiosity, gossip, intrusion. Her sense for the whole may easily lead to a scattering of her forces, to an aversion to the disciplining of her powers, to a shallow sampling of many fields, and to a possessiveness that goes far beyond genuine, motherly care. From flexibility to slavishness; from the power of bringing things together, of seeing both this and that, to ambiguity; from kinship with pain to whining; from the genius for friendship and alliance, to narrowness, partisanship and fanaticism — such are the penalties for an unhealthy exaggeration of woman's virtues. The sympathetic companion becomes an intruder who does not allow persons and things to ripen in peace and silence, and there is petty domineering where there ought to be the joy and strength of service. (From J. Oesterreicher, *The Walls are Crumbling*)

As a remedy against these weaknesses, Edith Stein suggests that a woman should engage in intellectual work, which serves as an antidote to the excessively personal, does away with superficiality and, because of its demand for subordination to objective criteria, is a school for obedience. Provided that she avoid the cult of specialization, intellectual discipline leads a woman to maturity and harmony; it gives her true culture and an authentic humaneness.

Of course, the special province of the woman is the home, but there are many areas outside the home in which she can fulfill her womanly calling: the field of medicine, teaching, social work, secretarial work or any task that requires sympathetic penetration into another person's thought, such as editing and translating. Even if she is forced by circumstances into a field that is not well suited to her feminine nature, such as working in a factory, a research laboratory or the military, a woman can still fulfill a role that is uniquely hers. In areas that are characteristically masculine, men can easily become less humane; but the presence and cooperation of a woman, with her concern for persons and wholeness, can be a counterbalance.

It should be evident that the attainment of mature manhood or womanhood presupposes a long and sometimes difficult process of development, of integrating the various sexual characteristics in both the wide and the narrow sense of the word. In the years of childhood, sexual differentiation is unobtrusive. A child may be curious about the bodily structure of the opposite sex, but once curiosity has been satisfied, there is hardly any further interest in sexual differences. The fact of being different is accepted as a more or less bothersome fact. To the boys, girls cry and tattle; to the girls, boys are rough and sometimes fight. From the age of about nine, boys and girls have their own activities and they go their own ways; to some extent they may even begin to confront one another. The boy often has more trouble in being a "boy" than the girl does in being a "girl" because the atmosphere of the home and family is largely determined by the feminine attitude of the mother. Nevertheless, both boys and girls of that age begin to identify with members of their own sex. Consequently, on the threshold of puberty the attitude toward the opposite sex is one of ambivalence, and it is aggravated by the lack of certainty about oneself.

In the years of puberty the biological sexual development is associated with sexual feelings that arise as a result of nocturnal emissions, spontaneous genital stimulation, or intense emotional arousal caused by fear, anger or physical exertion. Initially these feelings are not yet oriented to another person, but as boys and girls try to integrate these new experiences into their lives, they begin, strangely enough, to form intimate friendships with members of their own sex. Confidences are shared in this close relationship which does not tolerate a third person. These intensely human encounters derive their meaning from the need to discover the personality of the other as well as one's own personal identity. Such a friendship is in reality an experiment in love, and if the emotional lives of the individuals develop in a normal and healthy manner, they will progress to love for the other sex and the more matter-of-fact adolescent friendship. This process is, therefore, the preparatory stage of advancing to the other sex by way of a normal, ordinary friendship in which the previous ambivalent attitudes give way to a sincere interest in the other.

In their encounters with each other, adolescent boys and girls discover first of all how much men and women have in common, and this enables them to draw closer to each other. At the same time, there is an element of strangeness, of being different in spite of their closeness. The girl opens a new world for the boy and he sees to his amazement that it is not her way to be aggressive and to overcome obstacles, things that are so important to him and his friends. At first he is tempted to doubt his own manner of existence, but then he accepts it and at the same time admires the other world of the girl.

The girl, in turn, becomes fascinated with the boy's world. More and more they are drawn to each other, so that a new relationship develops between them, a relationship that is best described as one of tenderness born of respect. This tender, loving orientation towards the other leads spontaneously to the caress and the kiss, gestures which lend themselves so well to the expression of the desire to protect and safeguard the other. As a result, one no longer feels alone, but experiences the other as someone who helps to affirm his or her existence. The kiss and the caress stand, of course, on the threshold of genital sexuality, but this will not become a problem as long as the feelings involved are developed by way of the tenderness that signifies respect for the other and are controlled by the "restraining love" which I shall discuss later.

From this brief developmental sketch it is clear that the sexual differentiation of men and women is manifested and experienced under the increasing influence of psychic factors.

Genital sexuality loses its initially dominant determining force as other facets of the temperament, character and personality take on increasing importance. All of these facets are integrated into the stable and permanent adult personality by the most important development of all, which is not what is commonly called the "libido," but of human love.

Human Love

I believe that it is of the utmost importance that we understand the essential structure and the *modus operandi* of human love if we are to save ourselves and our children from much unnecessary man-made suffering which now plagues our unloving, sexualized world. The symptoms are evident: selfishness and frustration, excessive fear and utilitarianism, hate and indifference, atheism and the rejection of spiritual and moral values. Although exhortations to love are frequently heard, and rightly so, they often fall on deaf ears, simply because they are considered meaningless and pharisaical by persons who have never been loved, not even by those who brought them into this world.

The reason why human love is supposed to have such immense creative and healing power is not yet fully understood. This is due in great part to the fact that the entire emphasis has been placed on only one aspect or grade of human love while the other has been ignored or even directly or indirectly rejected and suppressed. As a result, our best efforts to love one another have proved futile and meaningless; instead of the intimacy of love expressed in warm personal relationships, we have the cold, businesslike structures for works of charity and the hand-outs from a welfare government.

What is human love? In general the word "love" signifies the feeling of attraction or, as St. Thomas Aquinas called it, the sense of affinity (*complacentia*) that one feels in relation to the good perceived in some person or thing. Whether a person experiences this affinity or attraction for the mountains or the sea, music or painting, a kitten or a puppy, one or another person, what is involved is a movement of the pleasure emotion called love. St. Thomas Aquinas rightly distinguished between sensory love (the emotion of love) and love as an operation of the will (volitional love). Ordinarily, however, people do not make a distinction between the emotion or feeling of love and the simultaneous movement of the will; they are not familiar with this distinction. They tend to identify all love with the "feeling" of love.

Nevertheless, whether they are aware of it or not, their love is always operative on two levels: the stimulation of the emotion of love and the concomitant movement of the will. The reason for this is that the person always reacts as a total human being, a substantial union of body and soul. Even our love for God should encompass both the emotions and the will, as Christ taught: "You shall love the Lord your God with all your heart, with all your soul, and with all your mind and strength" (Mk 10:30). Certainly the object here — God — is purely spiritual and as such, corresponds properly to our spiritual faculty of the will; but the individual should be disposed to experience a resonance of that love on the emotional level as well; otherwise we could not describe it as a truly human love.

Consequently, our love of God and of neighbor should be a love that is experienced in our whole being, including our sensitive being. If only the will is directed to the object of our love, our love is incomplete, imperfect, and falls short of the manner in which God wants us to love him and our fellow human beings. And although it is true that the emotion of love is a lower type of love than volitional love, it is nevertheless extremely important for the cultivation of mutual love between human beings. Normally we are not moved to love others or to be loved by them unless we and they can literally "sense" that love.

Here we touch upon the question of how these two types of human love are related to each other. As I have said, volitional love is the higher and more important because the human intellect surpasses all sense cognition and the human will surpasses all the emotions. The orientation of our will determines what we are as human beings. Thus, when our will is directed to God, when we have a spiritual love for him, our relationship is basically good, and we may say that we live in friendship with God. If, however, our will is averted from him because of a state of serious sin, we no longer have a spiritual love of God, no matter what our feelings otherwise may be.

The same is true as regards our love for our fellow human beings. When we will good for another person, we are exercising spiritual, volitional love for that person. This is possible even when we experience feelings of indifference or aversion for that person. Because of our volitional love, we will avoid doing what is evil or harmful to him; we may even do positive good for him, at least when duty requires it. Christ's commandment of love of one's enemy refers specifically to this volitional love, because a person who wishes us evil or actually causes us to suffer cannot be a good for our feelings as such. We can have a feeling of love for such a person only insofar as, in spite of being an enemy, we can find goodness in that person under some other aspect; for example, that he or she is a fellow human being or a brother or sister in Christ. But only the most mature among us, the most saintly, will be able to will and likewise *feel* love for our enemies.

Compared with spiritual, volitional love, the emotion of love is only secondary; it does not determine the very essence of our being or our spirituality. But this does not mean that emotional love is unnecessary, something we can just as well do without. On the contrary, even though emotional love belongs to a lower order, it is as much a part of the human being as is the will. As we have already said, love without concomitant emotional love is incomplete and defective. Emotional love belongs to the perfection of our human nature, and so much so that without it, a person is not fully human; an integral part of human nature is lacking. Indeed, without it, a person is incapable of obeying Christ's twofold precept of charity: love God and love your neighbor.

The reason for this is that a person's feelings of love determine one's rapport with others. We can initiate contact with others only through sense perception, and that involves the feelings. Volitional love, as we have stated, transcends the emotion of love and therefore cannot be perceived through the senses, although it may resonate on the level of emotional love. Consequently, unless the emotion of love comes into play, it is impossible to establish true human love between persons.

In order to analyze further the attraction of love, we must distinguish between selfish love and generous love. The attraction felt for someone or something may be stimulated in two different ways.

First, the good perceived in a person or thing may be directed to myself. I want to possess and enjoy it. I do not love the good for itself, but only insofar as it is pleasurable or useful for me. This is a self-centered love which reaches out to possess persons or things for one's own benefit. Such, for example, is the love of a man for a woman whom he desires only for sexual gratification. His love does not go beyond that and consequently he cannot love her as a person nor can he establish a true friendship with her. Similarly, in a purely utilitarian friendship, one person is attracted to another only for personal gain, and that too is a purely self-centered love.

Things are entirely different with generous love. In that case I love the other as a person. I do not try to draw that person to myself in order to possess and dominate, but I am drawn out of myself, so to speak, and to the other person (the original meaning of erotic love). That person is a good for me, to be sure, but not precisely because he or she serves a useful or pleasurable purpose. I do not seek myself in this relationship; rather, I desire the good for another, I desire well-being and happiness for the other. Not only that, but I am so much in union with the other person that I myself experience his or her sorrow and suffering, happiness and joy.

Generous love is primarily a volitional love, due to the fact that the spiritual faculty of the will enables the human person to be oriented toward the universal good and to the good of another. Emotional love, on the other hand, is essentially self-centered; of itself it cannot be generous and altruistic. For that reason, animals cannot love unselfishly. But generous love — volitional love — is what makes it possible for a person to step outside of self, so to speak, and to think first of the good of the other. Consequently, the love that should characterize the rational animal, the human being, is generous love, the love of friendship. Only then can an individual live up to Christ's command that we love one another.

That is the purpose of our existence: to attain to the perfection of generous love. What makes it so difficult for us to reach that goal is the fact that our nature is wounded as a result of original sin. We readily tend to be selfish, to seek our own good in preference to that of another. Only gradually and sometimes over a long period of time is a person able, with the help of God's grace, to become firmly rooted in the generous love which St. Thomas Aquinas calls *amor amicitiae* (friendship love). But once again it is important to realize that we should love both God and neighbor as total human beings, and therefore we should love with both our will (volitional love) and feelings (emotional love).

The Emotion of Love

Let us now answer the question: how does emotional love operate and develop? First of all, the emotion of love is normally operative long before volitional love. In the early years of life the human being is a predominantly sensate being whose intellect and will are still, as it were, in a state of latency. It takes some years before the intellect acquires sufficient abstract knowledge so that it can rise above the level of sensate cognition. The same is true as regards the will, and many years must pass before volitional love can serve as a guide and control of emotional love. Ideally, volitional love should develop in harmony with one's intellectual capability, but it is a fact that in the developmental process emotional love is operative long before volitional love emerges. In time, however, emotional love should be under the control of reason and will, so that in time the individual can develop an integrated, mature personality.

Like every other feeling, love is something that must develop gradually in every individual. This is possible only when from its very first days the infant experiences that another person (normally its mother) constitutes a good for it. The baby gets this experimental knowledge through the senses, and primarily through the sense of touch, the tactile sense. Caresses, kisses, hugging and cradling, coming from another person, and especially the mother, are the first and most important experiences of pleasure and of being loved. They are important because they affirm the baby; they make the baby more secure in his or her existence; they make the infant feel that he or she is good and therefore worthwhile. With the development of the other senses, the baby also experiences the mother's love in her affectionate gaze and in the gentle tone of her voice; then, later on, in her words of love and affirmation. But all through the years the tactile expressions of love remain important, although they will change in order to be properly suited to the various chronological stages of the child's development.

All the sensate manifestations of parental emotional and volitional love are perceived by the child as pleasurable and they arouse a feeling of love for the parents that has nothing to do with any utilitarian motives. The more the child senses that he or she is loved in this generous manner, the more the child is able literally to sense, to feel another human being as a good, and hence to develop a love for that other.

And how is this human love expressed? Again we must distinguish between volitional love and the emotion of love. As the expression of a sense appetite or emotion, emotional love is characterized by its own psychic and somatic aspects. Every emotion has its own psychosomatic reaction and manifestation. These comprise certain physiological changes that affect circulation of the blood, heartbeat, respiration, posture, facial expression, color of the skin, tone of the voice, etc. The reason for this is that *psyche* and *soma* (soul and body) are the elements of the substantial union of the human person and they can readily influence each other.

The psychosomatic reactions, for example, of fear and anger are well known to us, but those of the emotion of love quite often are not. The emotion of love is manifested in a person's appearance, in the way in which he or she looks at another, in the warm, pleasant tone of voice, in the way one shakes hands, in the aura of kindness and friendliness that he or she radiates. Of course, these manifestations or expressions of the emotion of love will be conditioned by such factors as personal temperament, sex, race, nationality, culture, family background and environment. These factors not only modify and condition the psychosomatic reactions and expressions, but they may sometimes cause them to be completely repressed.

It should also be noted that the psychosomatic reactions will also differ according to the type of love that is experienced.

Thus, the typical psychosomatic reaction of the feeling that accompanies generous love is *tenderness*, whether expressed in the softness of a caress, the warmth of the tone of the voice, or the gaze of love. Such tenderness is delicate and fragile; it respects and reverences the other, leaving him or her whole and intact, because such love is generous and unselfish.

It is quite another matter with self-centered love, which also has its own psychosomatic reactions. In this case, however, one person seeks to take possession of another, as it were; the beloved is used rather than loved unselfishly. Thus, the caress or the kiss on the hand, the forehead or even the lips, which is an expression of generous, benevolent love, is totally different from the caress or the kiss that is prompted by lust. In the latter case, instead of tenderness and respect for the person, there is possessiveness and sometimes the raw desire for self-gratification. So it is with all the tactile expressions of these two kinds of love; they are essentially different, and anybody with well-developed feelings is immediately aware of the difference.

The feelings that accompany generous love do not stop at the psychosomatic reactions; they stimulate voluntary motor reactions in relation to the person who is loved. One desires to make one's love known and felt; one wants to do what is good for the other; one wants to make the beloved happy or to take away sorrow and pain; to satisfy his or her every need. All this is simply an extension of one's feelings of generous, benevolent love and for that reason such a love is the natural source of all harmony and friendship among human beings.

Purely volitional love, on the other hand, does not necessarily cause any psychosomatic reaction. It may be an entirely spiritual act without any physical effects. For example, a person may love God or even another human being without any noticeable physical changes. It is only when the feelings participate in the act of volitional love that there will be any psychosomatic reaction, but then the reaction will be due to the emotion of love and not to volitional love as such. Moreover, generous volitional love may prompt a person to perform acts of charity and benevolence for another person or to work for the welfare of others. And all this may be done without any feelings of love, but only because one considers it right and proper to do good to others. This is possible because, unlike the animals, that are moved to action only by their passions, in human beings the will can transcend the emotions entirely. But here again, there is a difference in the voluntary motor actions that proceed from generous love and those that proceed from self-centered love. The former are done for the good of another; the latter are done for one's own good.

Having seen how these two types of love are manifested, we now ask how they are perceived by another person.

In the case of purely volitional love, as we have just stated, it will not necessarily be accompanied by any physical manifestation. Consequently it cannot be perceived by another person unless and until there is a concomitant or consequent movement of the emotion of love.

On the other hand, the emotion of love, like all the emotions, is always accompanied by some psychosomatic change, however slight. It is therefore normally perceptible to another person, and especially to the senses of sight, hearing and touch. Vision perceives the expression of love in the eyes, the smile or the coloring of the skin; hearing perceives the words of love and endearment or the tender tone of the voice; touch perceives the caress and the kiss. And all these physical changes are interpreted by the beloved as signs and expressions of love. Indeed, one can sense whether a caress or a gentle touch proceeds from real love and genuine affection or is simply an action proceeding from the will, as when one touches or caresses the sick for therapeutic reasons. A person may will to perform many acts that are normally the expression of the feeling of love, but a truly sensitive person is never deceived or misled in this matter.

Thus, one may be able to tell whether sexual caresses and stimulations are the manifestations of truly generous love or of selfish desire.

What then is the reaction on the part of the individual who is the recipient of the sensible manifestations of love? If the recipient perceives that the manifestations proceed from an authentic generous love that affirms the recipient in his or her existence, then that constitutes a sensed good for the recipient. Normally this will evoke a reciprocal feeling of love for the person who has already expressed his or her love. When expressed spontaneously and naturally, love usually calls forth a return of love and thus brings about the joy of loving.

We say that this normally happens, but not infallibly, because sometimes the mutual feelings of love are not aroused in the recipient. Whatever is received, says St. Thomas Aquinas, is received according to the manner or condition of the recipient. Thus, if the person who is the recipient of another's love is sad or antagonistic, he or she will not experience another's love as a good and therefore will not respond to that love.

Volitional love, as we have said, does not automatically arouse the feeling or emotion of love in the one who is loved. Even the good deeds that flow from another person's love for us do not necessarily touch our feelings. We may know intellectually that the other person desires our good, that he or she loves us spiritually, but this is on the intellectual level. It may awaken in us a sense of gratitude that may or may not be expressed in words, but it does not of itself stimulate the feelings of love.

This is of great importance for understanding our attitude toward God. We may have a firm belief that we have received everything from God and that God is our ultimate good, but that does not necessarily stimulate a feeling of love for God. It may in fact leave us emotionally as cold as a stone; we may even have a feeling of aversion toward God under some aspect or other. A true feeling of love for God can come about only when the emotion of love can somehow share in our spiritual love for God. But that presupposes that we are capable of emotional love. A person who lacks this capacity can never fully experience a real human love for God because the spiritual love does not reverberate throughout the rest of his or her being. Such a person cannot love God with his or her "whole heart, soul, mind and being."

Similarly, the lack of emotional love on the part of parents whose genuine volitional love causes them to do everything for their children explains the coldness and indifference that some children, and especially adopted children, sometimes display toward their parents. All the many good things that their parents did for them failed to touch their feelings, and in children the feelings are the principal stimulators of their actions and reactions. They may be grateful to their parents out of a sense of duty, but sometimes it is also accompanied by a sense of resentment. This happens simply because the parents gave no expression to emotional love for their children. Not that they acted this way deliberately — in fact, they may have done so unconsciously — but nevertheless an important ingredient of parental love was lacking. By this time it should be evident that if the relationship between people is to be a source of joy and happiness, their love for each other has to be expressed not only as volitional love, but also as emotional love. But now the question arises: in what manner will the expressions of emotional love be manifested?

The answer to this question can be stated as follows: in order to be truly *human*, the expressions of emotional love should always be in accordance with reason. As such, the emotion or feeling of love is a good because it is proper to human nature to love others. But it does not follow that each and every manifestation of emotional love is proper and reasonable. Like every other human act, it must be good in every respect, and as regards the expression of love, this means that it should be in accordance with the relationship that exists between the person who loves and the recipient of that love. Moreover, there may be circumstances in which certain manifestations of love, though good in themselves, are not prudent and must therefore be avoided. Reason must be the guiding and controlling factor here.

Something that is frequently overlooked in this context, however, is that reason must allow the feeling of love to retain its own psychosomatic reaction, its own natural expression; otherwise the feeling loses all its spontaneity. When the feeling of love — and any other human feeling — has been truly integrated into the personality through the guidance of reason, the manifestations of emotional love will automatically be in accordance with reason. This may not be true for the very first stirrings of feelings, of course, because there can be spontaneous movements of the emotions prior to any intervention of reason and will. Yet, once the feelings are stimulated in a truly mature and integrated person, reason will immediately take control. If, however, the individual has not yet achieved this integration of emotions and reason, it may be necessary to curb the expressions of the emotions in order to prevent what would be excessive under the circumstances.

But the controlling action of reason must never go so far as to interfere with the spontaneity of the emotional expressions. Then there would no longer be an expression of what can be felt by the other, but only something willed, something completely lacking in feeling or emotion. The individual ceases to be fully human and may even cease to be a good Christian, because to be a Christian means first of all to love.

This, then, is the first requirement as regards the role of reason, a negative one of not intervening too much. The second requirement is a positive one: that of deciding whether a given expression of the feeling is proper to the circumstances. One expresses one's feelings for a man differently than for a woman; an older person will have psychosomatic reactions that differ from those of a child or adolescent; one's behavior with a subordinate is different from that with a superior; etc. Prudence, the virtue of maturity, will show the right way and will provide a sense of what is too much or too little, proper or improper.

Prudence will do this provided we have no false, preconceived ideas on the subject; for example, that it is always wrong to touch another person; that rough-housing among boys is a moral danger; that kissing one's own son may lead to effeminacy; that all kissing among family members should be omitted. It is evident that where these and similar notions prevail, it is impossible to make a prudent judgment.

Special consideration must be given to love between a man and a woman. Here it is always possible that expressions of affection may arouse the sexual drive to such an extent that it demands gratification. In marriage there is no objection to such expressions; in fact, they will serve to unite husband and wife more closely. But outside the marital union, reason and prudence require that a man and woman abstain from manifestly sexual expressions of affection. Otherwise feelings will be aroused that cannot or should not be gratified in the normal fashion, and this can cause psychic tensions that disturb one's equilibrium.

In the case of an engaged couple, it would seem that the desirable development toward union should allow for certain expressions and manifestations that are sensual in character, yet even here it is necessary to avoid those that are too exclusively sexual. The period of engagement is aimed first of all toward the development of true love, generous love. This love is expressed not only in the sexual union but also by abstaining from everything that is improper in this regard. Even before their marriage the man and woman can develop the "restraining love" which is a mark of maturity and will be so important later on if their married life is to succeed. I shall have more to say about the love of restraint later on.

6

MISDIRECTED SEXUALITY

Masturbation

In direct contrast to the traditional opinion of theologians, who held that masturbation is always a serious sin, perhaps even more so than fornication, there is today in the Western world an ever growing tendency to claim that if not a morally good act, masturbation is at least a morally indifferent act. This opinion is held by lay and professional persons alike, and more recently even by some of the clergy, although not by the majority of any group.

Especially among psychiatrists not a few are found who consider adolescent masturbation a natural factor in the development of the human personality. Some psychiatrists would even diagnose its total absence as indicative of arrested psychosexual development. Thus, the Catholic psychiatrist Frederick von Gagern stated: "Self-abuse is in accordance with normal development at the introverted stages of early puberty, forit is a symptom of immaturity. Many psychologists are of the opinion that the young practice self-abuse without any idea of guilt, unless they have been told of its mortal sinfulness" (*The Problem of Onanism,* p. 97). Von Gagern seems to be saying that masturbation, while objectively wrong, is inevitable in adolescence as a result of the growing process and is therefore normal in adolescence.

The "natural" theory of masturbation, favored by so many psychiatrists, is based on Freud's teaching that the sexual instinct, the libido, is the primary developmental factor in man, and proceeds from infantile sexuality through adolescent masturbation to the fulfillment of human sexuality in adult life. In other words, it is the sexual instinct that determines the human personality, and it must not be interfered with by theologians who claim universally that masturbation in its objective morality is directly opposed to the Christian moral code. In fact, this school blames religion for causing transient, developmental masturbation to become a compulsory habit in adolescents. Since religion places undue stress on the sinfulness of masturbation, this can cause conflicts that will lead to mental illness in adult life.

There are also unwarranted statements by some moralists to the effect that in many cases of habitual adolescent masturbation the individual lacks the freedom and control that are necessary to make this act a mortal sin. There is some truth in this, but I would rather consider the immaturity at this age level, the lack of integration of the emotions with reason and will, and certain environmental factors, rather than the habit of masturbation itself.

It is true that masturbation may be said to be "normal" if we are concerned only with statistics, because they do tell us that the average adolescent masturbates at some time or other. But no rule of logic allows us to conclude from the frequency of masturbation that it is therefore normal in the development of the human personality. And even though some psychiatrists claim that the absence of masturbation is a sign of arrested psychosexual development — as in the case of neurotics who repress the sexual drive and all or most of its manifestations during the period of adolescence — this does not justify the conclusion that masturbation is a healthy, natural and normal developmental process. Rather, it must be compared to the stumbling and falling of an infant just learning to walk. The falls are "normal" only because this is the way practically all infants learn how to walk. The stumbling and falling are still defects in the process of walking correctly.

In addition to this, the claim that the fantasies that accompany the act of masturbation help the adolescent to form proper heterosexual relationships later on adds nothing to the argument that masturbation is natural and normal. The fact that he calls up fantasies of a partner of the opposite sex does not change the autistic nature of this act of misdirected sexuality. For that is what masturbation really is: misdirected sexuality; it is directed to self-gratification rather than to another person. Even when he fantasizes, the masturbator is concentrating on himself and his own pleasure, not on another person; in fact, by masturbating he excludes the other. Consequently, instead of helping the adolescent to give himself to another person, the habit of masturbation makes this gift of self more and more difficult. In extreme cases of predisposed persons it can eventually lock the individual in the fantasy world of the psychotic. But even when this happens, it was not primarily or exclusively because he masturbated habitually; it was also because he did not know how to love. Perhaps others did not make it possible for him to love, or he was not loved by others in his formative years, when their love could have stimulated a response of love on his part. When a child or adolescent is reared in such a way that the road to "the other" is closed to him, he can easily become fixed in the practice of masturbation as a surrogate for the "I-thou" relationship. He becomes introverted in his loneliness, having failed in his efforts to develop his sexuality in the wider sense of the term. The failure to go out of himself is further aggravated by the repeated acts of masturbation, and this sets up a vicious circle of frustrated desire and dissatisfaction, because he is engaged in an activity that is defective in its physiological and psychological aspects.

Masturbation also disrupts one's psychic harmony and integration because it focuses on the sexual sphere out of all proportion to the other human faculties. More and more the sexual instinct overrides reason as the practice becomes more frequent, with the result that it can distort the personality development. The lower faculties are no longer subservient to the reason and will; selfish preoccupation with sex prevents the individual from being open to the truth of reality and from finding satisfaction in the unselfish love for another. This is the grave consequence when educators condone the practice of masturbation as a natural process of development. Such persons are blind to the real needs of the adolescent; they fail to come to his help in trying to form authentic loving relationships with others.

On the other hand, although priests must be concerned with the difficult question of subjective morality in the confessional, the difficulty in forming a judgment in individual cases should not cause them to lose sight of the penitent's psychological needs. A harsh condemnation would only add to the adolescent's problem in going out to others in authentic love and would most likely intensify the habit of masturbation. The priest should realize that very likely other people — and possibly he also — have failed to encourage the penitent to go out to others and have thus indirectly contributed to the individual's habit of masturbation. Above all, the priest should establish a good relationship with the penitent so that he can discuss the problem with confidence and trust. The confessor should give the penitent counsel, but he should not attempt to set up a psychotherapeutic relationship, which is impossible to handle in the confessional.

In forming a judgment concerning the subjective morality of masturbation, the confessor should consider the age and the stage of emotional development of the individual. A certain awareness of the home environment would also be helpful. The confessor should also realize that the emotional life of the child or adolescent is chaotic; it consists of successive or simultaneous varied, and sometimes contradictory, emotions and impulses. This is so because of the disappearance of the regulatory system which is operative between the ages of about 7 to 10, when any impulse immediately stimulates an opposite reaction that balances out the former. But now, in this later stage, the will is dominated by impulses and emotions, and the adolescent must now begin to strengthen his will power. His actions are determined to a great extent by a combination of value concepts and ideas from the adult environment, but they are far from stable and clear. Nevertheless, they do give the will its motivation and an unconscious emotional identification. At the same time there is an increase in dreams and in the activity of the imagination. This can readily lead to the enjoyment of egocentric sexual acts. In addition to this, the increased activity of the glands that produce the growth and sex hormones will cause greater sensitivity and excitability in the genital organs.

Because of the instability of the newly developing regulatory functions in the years of puberty, and the physiological and psychological changes that prevent the adequate integration of emotions and will, it is possible that the habitual adolescent masturbator will rarely be capable of serious sin. However, even if this be true, we should not conclude that it is unnecessary to be concerned about acts of masturbation or that they are natural and necessary. On the contrary, we should see them as signs that the adolescent needs help in integrating his genital sexuality with his total sexuality.

Educators should recognize the danger of an inopportune, excessive moralizing attitude toward young people who already sense intuitively that certain behavior is improper. It is untrue to say that the majority of young people do not possess this intuitive knowledge or sense of shame and guilt. What happens is that their need to love and be loved is so intense that the intuitive sense of guilt is repressed, as in the case of individuals whose affective needs have been seriously frustrated. Later on, however, when the adolescent clearly and fully realizes that masturbation is morally wrong, the feelings of guilt will return with greater intensity.

A generally sound approach that educators can use is to tell young people that masturbation does not make sense and it leaves them dissatisfied anyway. Later, when they are able to discuss the matter further, they can explain to the young people that the reason why masturbation does not give them a real sense of satisfaction is that they are not sharing this activity and pleasure with anyone else. Gradually the adolescent will begin to understand that love and sex are not meant to be directed entirely and exclusively to oneself; they are supposed to be shared with another.

Thus, instead of giving a technical explanation of the physical and biological aspects of sexuality or a moralistic lecture on the sinfulness of masturbation, the educator should open the hearts and minds of adolescents to values such as friendship, love, truthfulness, respect and sympathy. In this way the educator will help young people to give meaning to their sexuality as an expression of their love for another person rather than as an evil to be avoided or a sin to be rejected.

In the selection of candidates for the priesthood and religious life special attention should be given to those individuals in whom frequent masturbation persists after adolescence. The following observations should be carefully noted:

1) If masturbation occurs in an individual who is very egocentric, emotionally unstable and unpredictable, it is likely that he would be diagnosed by a psychiatrist as a psychopathic personality or at least as a person with marked psychopathic traits. Such individuals should be judged to be absolutely unfit for the priesthood or religious life.

2) Compulsive masturbation is frequently a symptom of the obsessive-compulsive neurotic or scrupulous person. Usually there has been a repeated, long-standing repression of the sexual drive and its associated feelings because of fear or emotional energy. Consequently, reason and will are unable to perform their natural function of guiding and controlling the sex drive, which eventually manifests itself in obsessions or compulsions of a sexual nature. Only after the neurosis has been cured through psychotherapy can the fitness of the candidate be determined.

3) Masturbation as well as homosexual feelings should alert the vocational director to the possibility of a frustration neurosis. If such is the case, and if it is severe, this is an absolute contraindication of fitness for the priesthood or religious life. Persons with this type of neurosis suffer from intense feelings of inferiority and inadequacy. They develop deep depressions and are unable to assert themselves because of their strong but frustrated need to feel loved and accepted. Misinterpreting this latter need, males are sometimes led to believe that perhaps they should have been a woman, and from that they draw the mistaken conclusion that they must be homosexual.

4) Frequent masturbation may also be a symptom of early or latent schizophrenic psychosis, in which case the person should not be admitted to the seminary or religious life.

5) If frequent masturbation is the result of physical or psychological trauma, one must be guided by two factors: first, the earlier in life this trauma occurred, the less fit the person is for priesthood or religious life; second, the more

serious the trauma was, both subjectively and objectively, the less fit that person will be for a priestly or religious vocation.

6) Finally, frequent masturbation may occur in strongly concupiscible personalities, persons with intensely active emotions, who are capable of experiencing intense joy and also deep sorrow. If they can eventually control the sexual urge with ease and contentment, they may be admitted to the seminary or religious life; but if this proves to be too heavy a burden for them, they should not be accepted.

As an overall rule, in case psychiatric advice is not available, frequent masturbation — several times each week or even daily — is a contraindication for admission to religious life or the priesthood.

Homosexuality

As explained previously, boys and girls on the threshold of puberty begin to make friendships with others of the same sex, when they are not yet self-confident enough to approach the other sex. If for some reason a boy is afraid of encounters with the opposite sex and remains oriented toward his own sex, he may become a homosexual. Generally, the homosexual finds it hard to step out of the environment in which his own sex predominates and dares to do so only to a minimal degree.

One of the reasons for being afraid of the other sex may be found in his having been conditioned in childhood by a puritanical environment that prompts the individual to repress anything sexual and sensual and to consider any attraction to another person as a danger. Later on, this repression may develop into an obsession, with sexual fantasies and compulsive masturbation. Such persons become oriented by default to members of their

own sex because for them the opposite sex is even more dangerous. Although this situation causes guilt feelings and still more
repression, ultimately such individuals will take refuge in other
persons who have similar interests and usually similar fears.

Very often the fear of encounters with the other sex is
accompanied by hatred and scorn of the opposite sex. This is
even true for the effeminate male homosexual, who is commonly
but mistakenly believed to be desirous of being a woman, or as
much like a woman as possible. His effeminate behavior, man-
nerisms and dress are the result of having joined the feared
enemy in childhood as a defense against being defeated by them.
Although the majority of male homosexuals have not gone to
such lengths and have remained outwardly masculine in appearance, their reason for not going out to women is the same: hate
and fear. There is no doubt in my mind that this attitude is at the
root of the development of this psychological disorder in the
great majority of male homosexuals, at least in our Western
culture. Together with some minor contributing factors, it ac-
counts for the abrupt upswing in male homosexuality in recent
times; the same is true of female homosexuality, the incidence of
which probably parallels that of male homosexuality but in a less
spectacular manner.

There is some evidence — [Editor's Note: *Dr. Baar's
comments here are offered without in any way prejudicing the role of
genetics or other environmental factors which may, as well, contribute to the development of homosexuality*] — to indicate that the
emotional climate of the home in which the male homosexual
very frequently develops is one in which the mother is a
stereotypical "feminist" who is perhaps unconsciously hostile to
men. She is the dominant personality, the head of the house,
while the father is weak and passive, having surrendered his
natural position as head of the family to the wife, out of fear of
her aggressiveness, contempt and ridicule. He spends as much

time as possible away from the home or, what is usually the same, watching television and ignoring the family.

Such a mother is the key figure in the development of her son's homosexuality because, in her hostility to men, she seeks security — and perhaps revenge — by emasculating the men in her life. With her son she does this most frequently and effectively by "smothering" him with her "love." She breaks up his friendships with others his own age because he might get hurt playing games, or because the girls are not good enough for him, or because he needs his rest and must therefore always be home early. She is possessive, jealous and demanding in her manner of loving. Everything she does to protect her boy is done out of "love" for him, and she does this in such a manner that he feels guilty if he disappoints her in any way. She displays her disapproval in a non-verbal manner: a sigh, a shaking of the head, a hurt look, or wiping away a tear. These are more effective in keeping her son under control than any amount of scolding or physical punishment. It is also an effective way of conveying her contempt for her husband, for she may tell her son to respect his father, and then demonstrate by a smirk, a condescending smile or her silence that she herself does not.

If the mother succeeds in isolating her son from other people by the intangible barrier that she calls her "love," the boy becomes fearful or even hostile. He does not recognize these immediately repressed feelings, of course; he consciously believes that he loves his mother completely. At the same time he senses subconsciously that his mother does not constitute a good to which his feelings are attracted. The road to her and to all women is blocked by his unconscious fear and hostility. If his need to go out to others is strong enough, the only road is to persons of his own sex.

It is also possible that the boy will become aware of his feelings of fear and hostility because the mother did not or was not able to disguise her contempt for the men in her life by expressions and acts of smothering love. In that case the boy may become an aggressive bully in his attempt to prove that he is not a sissy or, on the other hand, he may surrender to his fear and become weak, passive, compliant, eager to avoid unpleasant scenes, leaving all decisions to others so that he can never be blamed. If later on he marries, such a boy becomes the prototype of the father whose sons are likely to become homosexuals.

The bullying, abusive father is basically a weakling who takes out his frustrations in alcohol and in the browbeating of his defenseless children. Fearful of his wife, he represses his anger and hostility, only to explode and curse from time to time the only persons he dares to punish and deride — his own children.

The weak and passive father, however, avoids the responsibility of assuming leadership in his family and takes little or no interest in his son's activities, ambitions, ideas or feelings. If he tries to assert himself at all, because of a sense of guilt, he will do so in an angry tone or by childish outbursts and unreasonable demands.

With either type of father, the son's natural need to identify with a strong, truly masculine father is thoroughly frustrated. He will repress his own aggressive, self-assertive and competitive inclinations, thinking they belong only to a woman. He becomes utterly confused in his relationship to either sex and becomes an easy victim of masturbation, homosexuality and, above all, loneliness.

Even the father who is absent through death, desertion or divorce can still exert an unfavorable influence on his son and contribute to his homosexual orientation. This happens when he is recalled in the boy's imagination with bitterness and resentment for any and all of the traits that I listed previously as typical of the immature, non-masculine, pseudo-masculine, passive and ineffective father. Even if the son never knew his father personally, this same imagination may be stirred if the mother often speaks of him in a degrading, ridiculing and spiteful manner.

She thus effectively emasculates the father and all men in the mind of her son.

[Editor's note: *Some of what Dr. Baars has stated here is debated and, though incisive, remains inconclusive. An excellent discussion on the deficiences in modern man and woman is to be found in Steve Clark's excellent work,* Man and Woman in Christ *(1980). He states that there are two types of men who have a problem in being men: the socially disruptive, excessively aggressive man (the "macho" type) and the "feminized" man (not necessarily homosexual). As regards problems of womanliness, he mentions three types of women for whom Christian femininity is a problem: the excessively submissive woman who suffers great insecurity because of her exaggerated dependence on others; the "masculinized" woman, who has learned to act and behave in ways that are more appropriate to men (not necessarily a lesbian); and the "feminist," who has been influenced by the feminist movement to compete with men and strive for equality with, if not superiority over men in every way.*]

Prevention and Treatment

From what I have discussed thus far it should be evident that the prevention of homosexuality is much more effective than any type of treatment or therapy. According to the most conservative estimate, approximately 2 to 6% of the population is homosexual; and in that case, individual treatment is a practical impossibility. Moreover, only a very small percentage of homosexuals seek help, and then, only when their homosexuality becomes a burden too heavy to carry or when they come into conflict with their relatives, church or society. Of this small group very few are interested in becoming heterosexual; most of them want to remain homosexual but make a better adjustment in their personal or social lives. Others have come into conflict with the law and are mandated by the courts to seek psychiatric help. These are usually pedophiliacs or those who seek sexual gratification with minors, because in many countries homosexual activity is not illegal between consenting adults, and in some countries the age of consent may be as low as 16 or 17.

The oldest form of treatment of homosexuals is punishment, but its results have been nil. The threat of punishment may strengthen the homosexual's fear of social or legal conflict but it will not change his homosexual orientation nor will it transform him into a heterosexual. Neither will the homosexual orientation be corrected through hormonal therapy, which will only reduce the sex drive. Some persons have advocated marriage as a solution, but marriage is not a therapeutic measure, and certainly not for homosexuals. In fact, an unsuccessful heterosexual contact may cause an even stronger homosexual drive.

As regards the use of psychotherapy, it is of interest to note that Freud himself found it very difficult; it was successful only under the most favorable circumstances. The stronger the fixation because of repeated homosexual activity, the poorer is the prognosis. The goal of psychotherapy is to open the way to heterosexual relationships, not necessarily in the area of genital sexuality, but simply to remove the fear or hostility toward the opposite sex or the feelings of inferiority and inadequacy.

Some have advocated group therapy, which has proved successful in resolving problems in other areas of life. If through dialogue in a group the individual can get rid of the rationalization that homosexuality is a socially acceptable way of life, the newly stimulated anxiety may possibly arouse the desire to change one's way of life. Moreover, contact with a group can strengthen the homosexual's self-confidence, diminish his loneliness, and convince him that homosexual activity is a curable form of disordered behavior.

But if we are to make any progress in the attempt to reverse the present upward trend in overt homosexuality among young men, we must stress prevention. I have already discussed the various causative factors in the home, our society and our culture that contribute to the development of homosexuality. I wish now to add a brief outline of the positive factors that will contribute to a mature, well-adjusted personality.

If girls are to become feminine women and boys masculine men, we must halt the race for superiority between the sexes. Instead of competing with each other, men and women must cooperate with each other to complement and fulfill each other through unselfish love of one another. A boy finds the most favorable climate for psychological growth — sexual and otherwise — when he can love and trust his mother without fear of losing his freedom; he must experience her love as uncondi- tional and not coming with a price tag. When the mother's love is warm and tender, when she is understanding and firmly consistent in her discipline, when she is willing to let go of her son as he develops more independence and self-reliance, in short, when she is mature enough to practice restraining love, the boy will develop the masculine qualities of a similar love, of sacrifice and empathy.

The boy's innate desire to be a man must also be nurtured by a father who is emotionally strong and stable, the head of the household, respected by members of the family and by the community. A truly masculine father does not have to be an ardent hunter, fisherman or sportsman; in fact many men betray their weakness and immaturity by their unbalanced overem- phasis on these activities, on mere roughness and toughness and physical strength as proof of their masculinity. A genteel, quiet scholar can be as masculine as any athlete, and sometimes more so. He does not have to play football with his son to prove that he is a man, but he will do so to show that he is interested in his son and wants to establish a good relationship with his son. But the father manifests his good masculine qualities best of all when he shows good judgment and common sense; when he respects his wife and children, their ideas and feelings; when he functions as the head of the house in a democratic fashion.

If the father is absent because of death or for some other reason, the mother should speak of him always in a positive, respectful and admiring manner, even if her feelings are otherwise in his regard. If she emphasizes his masculine qualities as a father and remains silent about his shortcomings or possible faults, an absent father can still exert a positive influence on his son's development to maturity.

Sexual Education

It cannot be denied that in our culture sexual education is still a problem. We have not succeeded in integrating sexuality into the total life of our young people. One of the principal reasons for this seems to be that many educators (whether parents or teachers) find it difficult to be objective, perhaps because some of them since their childhood have been unsuccessful in integrating their own sexuality.

Christianity has always been concerned about sexuality, love, marriage and procreation. Throughout the centuries piety and pseudo-piety have declared war against the temptations of the flesh. Even St. Paul, who spoke so beautifully about marriage, seemed to miss the total reality of sexuality and to say in so many words: "Make the best of sex until the second coming of Christ." Unfortunately, too many failed to make the best of sex, as evidenced by Origen, who castrated himself because he did not know what to do about his sexuality; by the extreme ascetical practices of the Middle Ages that stimulated the very passions that the individuals wanted to control, and sometimes reached the level of sadism or masochism; by the scandal of sexual activity even on the part of the celibate clergy; by the failure to cultivate healthier ideas about sexuality after the Council of Trent, which did so much to improve seminary formation in other areas.

Manuals of moral theology and ascetical theology have also done much to promote the estrangement and antagonism between man's spiritual and physical nature. The harmful effects of this one-sided treatment of the human body-soul composite are not easily repaired. It is still difficult to convince people that taboos, far from destroying an evil, will sometimes foster and increase it. Children are naturally curious about their genitals, which are operative in their daily life, and adolescents will normally be interested in the changes that are occurring in their bodies and sex organs. But this natural curiosity can become an obsession if educators try to abolish it by threats, prohibitions, shame, warnings or by branding all sexual and sensual feelings as sinful. Thus, some moral theologians state that young people may "tolerate" the sexual feelings that may be experienced in wrestling, horseback riding, and other activities that may cause sexual stimulation. This is an implied condemnation of any and all sexual or sensual pleasure and it prevents young people from acquiring an open-mindedness and detachment concerning their own and others' bodies.

Moreover, attempts to help people gain control of their developing sexuality by excessive emphasis on will power, by challenging them to be "soldiers of Christ," or frightening them with the prospect of venereal disease or mortal sin leads to non-integration of their sexuality. That can be just as detrimental as the negative attitude of "Do as you please; we all have to go through this." In both cases the result is to focus the attention on the genital organs and act, implying that genital sexuality comprises the essence and totality of sexuality. This makes it impossible for the young person to understand and appreciate the role of sexuality in other areas such as the emotions and the will. Sexually mature men and women know from experience that sexuality involves the entire person. In other words, they know that their sexuality is experienced and expressed in other ways besides the genital sexual act.

The educator — and this applies especially to parents — should assist young people to reach sexual maturity by a sexual education that is integrated with the rest of the educational process. While clothing, hair style and toys, for example, do mark the sexual differences early in life, children should be allowed to make the distinction spontaneously and not be forced into it by premature and repeated stress on masculine and feminine characteristics. At first there will normally be a mixture of both the masculine and feminine qualities in a child and this should be tolerated for a time. As the children begin to associate more with their own peers, the sexual differentiation will become evident in a natural and easy manner. But if the first encounters with their own peers are unsuccessful, the educator will have to use a great deal of tact to help the child resolve this problem.

As the child grows, all questions about sex should be answered honestly and simply, but without detailed explanations. Young children are satisfied with much more simple answers than their questions may indicate. Premature descriptions of the mechanics and techniques of sex could be as harmful and inhibiting as awkward, ill-timed parent-child sex talks. Too often, because of the embarrassment of the parent, the child gets the impression that there is something wrong with sex and that it cannot be dealt with in a natural manner, even when grown up and married. Parents who are too embarrassed to give sex education to their children would do better to give them a reputable book that they can read for themselves.

Around the age of six a child normally begins to develop a sense of modesty, and this should be respected by adults, even if at times it seems excessive. This is an element of the more general need for privacy and it should be allowed to develop.

This is impossible, however, if the parents and other members of the family lack a sense of modesty or do not respect the privacy of others. Nudism practiced as a cult in the home or in groups outdoors is not a manifestation of impurity; it is an infantile practice that shows that the individuals have not yet been able to integrate nudity into their human existence.

If a parent happens to catch a child in the act of masturbating, he or she should refrain from shaming or punishing the child. Rather, this is an occasion in which the parent can discuss calmly, but in a manner suited to the child, the role of sexuality. By punishing the child, one might well precipitate intense guilt feelings that could lead later on to serious emotional inhibitions in the matter of sexuality. I once heard of a parent who caught his son masturbating and he took him down to the basement and opened the door of the furnace, where a fire was raging. He then told the child that he would burn in hell for all eternity if he ever played with himself again. This frightened the boy so much that he was cured forever of masturbation. He never again played with himself — only with other boys. He became an active homosexual.

On the other hand, parents who treat masturbation as a laughing matter, or with indifference, or even give tacit approval to the practice, are equally negative in their approach. They make it very difficult for their children to develop a reasonable and healthy attitude toward sex or to cultivate the will power and self-control necessary for integrating this drive with other non-sexual drives.

Because of the difficulty some youngsters encounter in this area, they may for a time experience an "existential uncertainty." Here again, the educator must be able to think and feel on the level of the young person if he or she is to provide meaningful and responsible assistance. The more closely the adolescent approaches maturity, the more differentiated his love for the other will become. This is a part of the healthy maturing process but it requires great tact on the part of the educator. It is at this point that serious mistakes are sometimes made, especially by parents, who submit the boy or girl to a cross-examination after being out with a member of the opposite sex, who make a false interpretation of their behavior, who are suspicious or make insulting or belittling remarks about the boy friend or girl friend. Such an attitude is an insult to the adolescent, who needs to be affirmed by the educator's confidence and to be given enough room in which to exercise some freedom and independence.

7

LOVE, SEXUALITY AND CELIBACY

What I have said previously about the importance of emotional love in general, namely, that without it volitional love is sterile and bears no fruit, is of special significance for those persons who are called to represent Christ among the People of God and to be instruments of his teaching and his sacramental graces. The more we experience the love of a priest for us, the more likely we are to accept and follow his teaching. The more we feel Christ's love for us, the more we will give him our love in return. This applies also in its own way to those who have embraced the consecrated life of the evangelical counsels: religious and members of secular institutes.

It is important that the priest possess a human love that encompasses the emotional as well as the spiritual. And with the growing awareness of the need for such love in a priest there is likewise an increasing effort to know more about this love and how it can be developed in candidates for the priesthood and the consecrated life. It has also raised the question of the necessity of celibacy for priests. Not, however, for those in the consecrated life, since they have vowed to live the evangelical counsels of poverty, chastity and obedience. Moreover, one may also ask which life is more conducive to the development of perfect human love, the married life or the celibate life, or whether it is even possible to have a fully developed love in the celibate life. In fact, the higher incidence of emotional and sexual difficulties that have come to light concerning priests in our day has given added weight to the arguments against celibacy.

The Priesthood

As regards the Catholic priesthood, one also hears an argument against celibacy based on the assertion that celibacy is a "charism"; therefore it should be chosen freely and not imposed by Church law. However, one suspects that this argument is simply a cover-up for those who want a married clergy in the Latin Church. Admittedly, there is a difficulty — more for some than for others — in integrating genital sexuality with pure love in the celibate state, whether the individual be a priest, a member of a religious or secular institute or an unmarried lay person. But the conflict between personal freedom and the authority of the Church is a non-existent one. Everyone knows that the Church asks each individual candidate to accept the celibate life voluntarily. This may limit the number of acceptable candidates for the priesthood, but there is no restriction of the freedom with which one embraces the celibate life. He may not be free to choose the priesthood or consecrated life without celibacy, but he does make a free choice. Similarly, the lay person is not free to choose a married state that is not permanently binding, yet this does not mean that he or she is not free in entering into an indissoluble marriage.

One would expect that the modern sciences of psychology and psychiatry would have something of value to contribute to this discussion, and so they do. But the psychologist and the psychiatrist must realize that they cannot have the last word on this subject; there are also biblical and theological aspects to be considered. In fact, one may wonder whether we would have been able to accept the celibate life as a meaningful mode of existence if Christ had not explicitly spoken of this possibility and if the Church had not approved this evangelical counsel throughout the centuries.

Consequently, the psychologist and the psychiatrist should recognize the positive value and meaning of celibacy as proclaimed in the biblical teaching. First of all, the statement of Christ when his disciples asked him whether it would be better not to marry: "Not everyone can accept this teaching, only those to whom it is given to do so. Some men are incapable of sexual activity from birth; some have been deliberately made so; and some there are who have freely renounced sex for the sake of God's reign. Let him accept this teaching who can" (Mt 19:10-12).

The second quotation is from St. Paul: "Given my preference, I should like you to be as I am. Still, each one has his own gift from God, one this and another that. To those not married and to widows I have this to say: It would be well if they remain as they are; but if they cannot exercise self-control, they should marry. It is better to marry than to be on fire. . . . The unmarried man is busy with the Lord's affairs, concerned with pleasing the Lord; but the married man is busy with this world's demands and occupied with pleasing his wife. This means he is divided. The virgin — indeed, any unmarried woman — is concerned with things of the Lord, in pursuit of holiness in body and spirit. The married woman, on the other hand, has the cares of this world to absorb her and is concerned with pleasing her husband. . . . I have no desire to place restrictions on you, but I do want to promote what is good, what will help you to devote yourselves entirely to the Lord" (1 Cor 7:7-9; 32-35).

This second text speaks of the celibate state as offering the opportunity to sit with the Lord quietly, undividedly and without distractions, as Mary of Bethany sat at the feet of Jesus. And although the priest is ordained for ministry to the People of God, the Church wants him to concentrate especially on the *unum necessarium* as did Mary of Bethany.

When considering which state of life is the most suitable for a priest from the psychological point of view, it is necessary first to determine the nature of the priesthood, what it means to be a priest. A priest is a clergyman, a cleric, and the word *klerikos* in Greek means portion or lot. In ecclesiastical usage it refers to the sons of Levi who, instead of receiving a parcel of the Promised Land, receive the Lord as their portion. The same idea is expressed in Psalm 16:5: "O Lord, my allotted portion and my cup, you it is who hold fast my lot."

In the Catholic tradition the priest is "another Christ," a mediator through whom Christ bestows his graces upon mankind. He is also the instrument through whom God speaks, the proclaimer of the Gospel. He is a shepherd or pastor who serves the faithful and leads them to God. He stands between God and man, and it is through him that God and man meet. Therefore, the priest does not exist for himself but, as God's instrument, he exists entirely for the priestly ministry; he is ordained for ministry. And like any other instrument, he must not place any obstacle or hindrance to the work or effect intended by the primary agent; rather, he must be finely attuned to the intentions of that primary agent (God) and at the same time perfectly adapted to the needs of the faithful he serves.

It is in the light of this understanding of the Catholic priesthood, of the priest as the mediator and meeting place between Christ and the faithful, that we can determine which state of life is most suitable for the priest.

Marriage vs. Celibacy

Would the married state constitute an impediment for the priest or an obstacle to his ministry? In an absolute sense, the priesthood is not incompatible with marriage. In fact, in the early Church celibacy was not obligatory for the priest, nor is it today in some of the Eastern Churches. Nevertheless, it was always highly regarded as an ideal and was observed by many priests, as it also is today in some of those same Eastern Churches. It seems that it was only when more and more priests remained celibate voluntarily that the Western Church, first at the Council of Elvira in Spain (between 300 and 303), made it a requirement for priests in the Latin Church.

[Editor's Note: *In 1967 both Pope Paul VI and the Synod of Bishops stated that the tradition of the Eastern Churches which permits the ordination of married men to the priesthood is to remain unchanged. However, no man may marry after priestly ordination and only celibate priests can be ordained bishops.*]

Ecclesiastical celibacy requires that priests in the Latin Church refrain from marriage and its procreative act as well as all voluntary sexual pleasure. It obtains its fullest meaning and value when this renunciation is an expression of a total, unconditional and loving dedication to the service of God and the People of God. Hence, it not only makes the priest free *from*, but more importantly, it makes him free *for*. He is free from the burdens and obligations of the married state so that he can be free to be "all things to all men."

If a priest were to be married, he would have as his first duty the care of his wife and children; his professional activity would have to be subservient to this time-consuming and attention-demanding prior obligation. This would be true even if the Church provided financial support for him and his family, for it takes a great deal of time and attention if a husband is to love his wife in a meaningful way and properly care for his children.

To give you some idea of what the husband means for the emotional life of the woman, I want to quote a famous line from Homer's *Iliad*. It is from Andromache's farewell to her husband Hector and it shows how well Homer understood the nature of a woman: "Hector, you are to me all in one: father, venerable mother and brother; you are my husband in the prime of your life."

The husband is the father who protects and defends the wife; in whose hands she knows she is safe and to whom she can always go when danger threatens. He is a mother who treats her with tenderness. He is the brother who is her companion and friend. All this is what the husband means to the woman; all this is what she expects from the man to whom she has entrusted her entire life.

Years of experience in psychiatric practice leave no doubt in my mind about the devastating emotional and mental effects on wife and children when the husband does not express his love for them in a meaningful manner. The wife may know intellectually that her husband is a good provider, is dedicated to his work, and does not pursue other women, but the female psychology is such that this is insufficient to guarantee her happiness or prevent emotional illness. She must also receive concrete sensate manifestations of his love that she can see, feel and hear. And because sense impressions are fleeting and last for a very short time, in contrast to the effect of reasoned, intellectual knowledge, they must be repeated frequently, consistently and in many varied ways, if the woman is to experience the joy of being loved. But this is impossible if the husband is away much of the time or is too absorbed in his own interests.

To ignore these basic psychological laws is to precipitate mental depression and emotional disturbance or prompt the woman to seek love and fulfillment elsewhere. Now, in the case of a priest-husband, it seems inevitable that in order to take proper care of the emotional, educational, social and medical needs of his family, he would have to use much of the time and energy that is needed for unselfish and devoted service to his flock. As we have seen, St. Paul was well aware of this fact.

Psychology of the Celibate State

The next question to be considered is whether the celibate state is an unnatural one. When Christ spoke of "those who have freely renounced sex for the sake of God's reign" (Mt 19:12), he was referring to those who renounce marriage and the use and pleasure of the sex act. But Christ also admitted that not all can accept this teaching. However, if marriage is the natural vocation of men and women, what about the claim that the celibate life prevents the development of the personality to full maturity and the establishment of deep affective relationships with other persons?

The presupposition that underlies that claim is that the mutual perfection and fulfillment that husband and wife give to each other is found in the performance of the marital act. But that is a false presupposition. A husband and wife bring about each other's existential fulfillment through their unselfish, mature love for each other. True, their mutual love often reaches its climax in the sexual act, provided they give themselves to each other completely, without holding back. But the sex act as such is not essential to the perfection of the partners; indeed, it is possible for a husband and wife to complement and fulfill each other in a marriage in which for some reason the sex act is never performed. On the other hand, there are marriages in which the sex act is performed very frequently, and yet little or no human perfection is seen in either spouse.

Of course, it cannot be denied that anyone who foregoes marriage is deprived of many opportunities for developing the emotional maturity and social sensitivity that are found in the intimacy of married life. But before concluding that it is therefore essential that celibates should marry, let us examine the development of a mature personality.

By the time a person enters into marriage, his or her emotional life should already have been developed to a great extent. It will still be necessary, of course, to cultivate a harmonious integration of the emotions among themselves and between the emotions and the higher operations of intellect and will. Then, under the influence of reason, the emotions will gradually lose much of their self-centered orientation and will more and more be aroused by the good of the other. In this way the originally selfish emotional love is elevated, as it were, to the level of generous, mature, human love, in which both emotional and volitional love are directed to the good of the other. Then the spouses will experience both in their feelings and in their will the joy of giving themselves to another.

When both partners in marriage have reached this stage, their love for each other is friendship love (*amor amicitiae*). And this friendship love, which is a restraining love, is the most important factor in regulating one's genital sexuality. Such a love can be developed in marriage, albeit not without difficulties and conflicts, if at the beginning of their married life the partners already possessed a reasonably harmonious, non-repressed emotional life, a capacity for altruistic love and concern for another, and an adequate subordination of genital sexuality to the higher faculties of intellect and will.

But is this friendship love (*amor amicitiae*) reserved only for married persons? Does the celibate life make it impossible for a person to become a mature and fulfilled human being? The answer to both questions is no. In fact, under the proper circumstances, the celibate life can even make it possible to attain this maturity at an earlier period in life.

Although the celibate deprives himself of the deepest possible intimacy with another person, he too can develop into a harmoniously balanced person who attracts others by his warm and radiant unselfish love. As a result, he too can experience the happiness that comes from being loved by others. But for this to happen, two conditions must be fulfilled. First, he must possess at the time of his commitment to celibacy the selfsame qualities we have just indicated for those entering marriage. Second, the whole environment of the seminary or novitiate, as determined by the regulations and schedule, the professors and staff, and one's peer group, must be such that the individual is not forced to repress and distort his emotional life but is encouraged to unfold and develop all the aspects of his personality in a wholesome, integrated manner. If, under such favorable circumstances — and later on in the priesthood or religious life — the seminarian or novice can constantly accept the lack of gratification of his natural desires for the sake of his freely chosen ideal and does not underestimate the sacrifice or judge genital sexuality as something universally sinful, in a neurotic attempt to make the sacrifice more bearable, he can attain the same degree of happiness and fulfillment that can be found in the married state.

Like his married counterpart, the celibate will experience difficulties and inner struggles, especially in the thirties and forties, when a man's drives and desires are usually the strongest. The fact that both married men and celibates experience these difficulties proves that their happiness and fulfillment have nothing to do with the gratification or non-gratification of the sexual drive; rather, it is simply a question of their ability to learn and practice restraining love. Further credence is given to the absolute importance of this love when one realizes that the celibate who is constantly aware of the noble reason for his choice of life will attain the maturity of restraining love and its concomitant joy earlier than the married man. The latter usually needs more time to reach that maturity.

Another consideration is the fact that when a man reaches middle age he usually begins to concern himself with more spiritual matters. He realizes the transitory nature of the things he has enjoyed and becomes more aware of life's approaching end. Consequently, he tends to devote himself more to that which transcends time and space. He also thinks more of others in society at large and is prompted to help them.

In contrast, the celibate priest or religious did not wait until the later years to cultivate a more spiritual orientation. As relatively young men, priests and religious devoted themselves to spiritual values and service of others, something the married man could not do because of his duties to his home and family and his involvement in temporal affairs. It is difficult to see, therefore, how the celibate life, accepted freely and with proper motivation, could be an obstacle to human maturity and fulfillment.

The well-known German psychiatrist, Richard Krafft-Ebing, stated in his *Psychopathia Sexualis* (1886): "It shows a masterly psychological knowledge of human nature that the Roman Catholic Church enjoins celibacy upon its priests in order to emancipate them from sensuality, and to concentrate their entire activity in the pursuit of their calling."

Notwithstanding the many positive effects of the celibate life, one may raise a final question concerning the advisability of requiring celibacy of all priests. Does the priest arrive at early spiritual maturity at the expense of retardation in the development of his lower faculties? In other words, are celibates emotionally immature; do they have more sexual conflicts than the married man?

My own experience in private psychiatric practice with numerous priests and men and women religious as well as unmarried lay people confirms the opinion of other knowledgeable writers, namely, that priests and celibates generally have neither more nor less sexual difficulties than married men. Of course, when sexual problems or scandals are reported in the life of a priest, they receive wide attention and cause consternation because people do not expect these things to occur in the life of a well-educated and highly respected individual. This, however, should not be interpreted as proof that priests have more sexual problems than married or unmarried laymen.

[Editor's Note: *The rate of incidence of heterosexual or homosexual activity, alcoholism; etc. is generally the same for all professional groups: clergymen, doctors, lawyers, professors, politicians, etc. Unfortunately, these are the cases that are widely reported in the communications media and make a deeper impression on the public.*]

All men are faced with the problem of integrating the strong and fundamental sex drive with their higher faculties of intellect and will. All men have to learn how to overcome self-centered love and be able to love another person with a generous, outgoing love. Whether that other is a woman, as in marriage, or Christ, the Church or one's fellow priests and religious in a celibate life, there is no essential difference. It is still a question of turning from love of self to love of another.

Indeed, to be a good priest or celibate requires as much masculine maturity and the same qualities as to be a good husband and father. If either one experiences his genital sexuality as the main focus of interest and concern, that very fact is an indication that he has failed to bring his lower faculties under the control of reason. As a result, he will tend to relate to another individual as an object of self-satisfaction or utility but not as a person worthy of love. Consequently, in both states of life a man must practice a restraining love that controls but does not repress the legitimate longing to love and to be loved.

When priests or married men fail, it is usually because their ability to love maturely has not yet developed. This may be caused by hereditary factors (as in the case of the psychopathic personality), an unconscious or environmentally determined impediment (repressive or frustration neuroses), or even a deliberate, self-imposed, but harmful refusal to develop the capacity to love (the result of improper formation and education). Generally speaking, a priest with emotional and sexual difficulties will not be helped by allowing him to marry, in the mistaken belief that it is the absence of a loving partner that caused his difficulties and conflicts. Since his real problem is his inability to make the gift of himself through love, he will still have that same difficulty in the married state. In this regard it is well to point out that the reluctance of the Church to dispense a priest from his promise of celibacy is as much of a blessing for him as the indissolubility of marriage has been for the Christian community. Many a priest would have failed to meet the challenge of the maturing process successfully if he had been dispensed from celibacy and allowed to marry.

Formation for the Celibate Life

How can the foregoing psychology of love and sexuality be incorporated into the education and formation of candidates for the priesthood and the consecrated life? The first question that arises, of course, is the minimum age for a boy to enter a seminary or religious novitiate. Is a boy of thirteen or fourteen old enough to make a responsible choice in the matter of his personal vocation? The fact that the drop-out rate for minor seminaries is 83% would seem to indicate that he is not. This is not surprising when one realizes that many college students in their late teens or early twenties are not able to make a definitive decision concerning their future state of life or profession.

Actually, the more fundamental question is whether or not the minor seminary, in cases where there is good reason for its existence, provides a favorable environment for the psychosexual development of the boy. From what I have said about this stage of personality development, one must conclude that the minor seminary is not a natural setting for the ultimate sexual differentiation that should occur at adolescence; it requires contact with the opposite sex. In some cases the drawback of a sex-segregated school can be compensated for by long summer vacations at home, but it must be remembered that seminaries, military schools and boarding schools can never replace the home. Home and family are the only natural setting for a youngster to develop a mature personality.

I have no idea why or when the minor seminary had its origin, but I would not be surprised if it was prompted by the fear of losing vocations if the boys were exposed to worldly temptations. In addition, there was the sincere but erroneous conviction that the repression of the emotional life in a secluded environment was necessary for the training of the will. If my suppositions are true, then our growing understanding of the positive significance of the emotional life for the spiritual life — although far from being accepted universally — should help us improve the overall climate of minor seminaries as long as it is not possible to close them. In fact, a closer study might conceivably come up with suggestions for improvements that would justify the existence of the minor seminary in a society in which family life is increasingly deteriorating.

The process of adaptation and renewal will necessarily be a slow one for several reasons, one of which is the fact that mere knowledge of the correct concepts of love and sexuality will not automatically make us or our young people mature. We have to start by controlling our overactive emotions of fear and energy, on which we have relied so long for becoming better Christians, and give our latent affective emotions some room for growth so that we can love a little more humanly. If we can do that, then today's children in school and catechism classes will be able to let their children grow into warmly loving and deeply spiritual human beings.

Instead of making abrupt and drastic changes which appeal so much to our overdeveloped utilitarian and energy emotions, we must calmly and deeply re-think our ideas of love and sexuality. We can start by correcting the contemporary attitude toward sexuality, which is interested only in emotional and sensate satisfaction, while its primary purpose, procreation, is considered incidental and, in many cases, not desirable. It is this thinking that has led to the belief that genital sexual gratification is a necessary condition for human maturity and that therefore any and all means for preventing conception should be supported. That this is fundamentally wrong needs hardly to be said. The sex act is and remains primarily an act of procreation; it is the sensate gratification and pleasure that are secondary.

Our primary task in the home and in catechism classes — and to a lesser extent in the minor seminary — is to emphasize the beauty and value of the procreative function and the sex act as an expression of mutual generous love. In this way youngsters can begin to see sexuality as a good that should be respected and appreciated. If they can understand that sensual gratification is a secondary aspect of sexuality, while procreation is its primary purpose, they will more likely avoid masturbation and, when they marry, they will more likely reject the use of contraceptives. Then, understanding that the purpose of the sex act is procreation, it will not be necessary to prove that the sex act should be restricted to marriage, since a child needs to be cared for and nurtured in a stable and secure environment.

This approach avoids the mistake that has been made too often and for too long, namely, presenting sexuality as something inferior, dangerous and an occasion of sin. Such an attitude will inevitably prevail when too much emphasis is placed on the sexual feelings or the sin of lust, instead of pointing to the infant as the fruit of love. As a consequence, one is led to concentrate on sexual feelings as the determining factor and thus develops abnormal tensions in regard to sexuality.

Not every priest, seminary professor or teaching religious will be able to convey the proper attitude towards sexuality, for the simple reason that so many of them have a lifelong history of sexual repression. It is not their fault and it must be tolerated for the time being. Perhaps it would be better, however, if such sexually immature persons would refrain from teaching religion and moral theology or giving spiritual direction, and leave these tasks to the more mature and well-integrated members of the staff. It is an undisputed but not generally known fact that educators cannot convey the full truth about love and sexuality unless they themselves are capable of feeling and expressing love. Feelings beget feelings, and the mature feelings of the educator will go a long way in helping youngsters and seminarians to complete their emotional maturation. The intellectual expertise of the educator or his or her admonitions to love do not suffice.

What I have said about the minor seminaries is also true for the major seminaries: the professors must be emotionally mature and know how to love, experiencing their sexuality in a controlled manner, and not as a repression. Their attitude towards friendships among the seminarians must be sound and healthy. And whereas minor seminarians should have ample opportunity to have contact with their family and friends of both sexes, the major seminarians should likewise have contact with the world. The extent to which such contact should be fostered will depend on the emotional maturity of the seminarians and the ability of the teaching staff to develop in them a sense of responsibility and obedience.

[Editor's Note: *Since the Second Vatican Council it has become more or less the general policy to provide contact with the "world" through pastoral apostolates that serve as a kind of internship for the future priest.*]

In conclusion, let me take a look at the mature priest, whether he is a seminary professor, a parish priest, or works in some other ministry in the diocese. First of all, such a priest *will* exercise volitional love, that is, the will to serve others without seeking his own good. This is the standard by which he will be judged to be a good priest. This, however, is not enough if his work is to be effective and fruitful. His spiritual love must also be expressed through feelings, because he can move others only through his feelings of love for them. No matter how convincing his statements concerning faith and morality, he will accomplish little without a warm and cordial rapport with each individual.

Of course, it is impossible for the priest — or any individual — to have a personal love for each and every person. He can never measure up to the love of Christ, which is infinite. Nevertheless, it is possible for the priest to have a "functional" love for people, a love that is expressed in dedicated service to his people. Fundamentally this is a volitional love, but one that is accompanied by feelings of kindness, compassion and affection. And he will have this if his emotional life is properly developed.

But the priest — like all human beings — also needs the love that is experienced in personal friendships. This love differs from functional love to the extent that in friendship he gives love to another and receives love from the other. Of course, he may also receive affection from others as a result of his functional love, but it will be an affection based on gratitude for what he has done or in reverence for his position as a priest. Actually, it is not a requirement for functional love that the priest receive love in return. A good priest will devote himself wth as much love to those who fail to respond as to those who show their appreciation and affection. In friendship love, however, the priest is in a sense on an equal footing with the other person, receiving love for love and experiencing the joy of being affirmed in love. We could say that friendship love is characterized largely by being loved and receiving love, while functional love is more a matter of giving through love.

Christ himself gave us the example in his friendship with Lazarus, Mary and Martha and St. John the Beloved. There is no reason why friendship love should exclude a member of the opposite sex; after all, the love between a man and a woman does not necessarily involve sexual activity. A priest may, of course, experience a sexual desire, but he must be able to control that urge by what I have called restraining love. And this can be done only by a priest who has harmoniously integrated his sexuality into his spiritual orientation. A priest who is not fully mature, both emotionally and spiritually, has no business cultivating a friendship with a woman. If he is not guided by a pure, generous human love, the selfish desire that springs from the sexual feeling will easily come to the surface and even take control, and this would do harm to the friendship. But a priest who is capable of a truly generous love and can express this love for a woman without sexual tension will develop an even warmer and more spontaneous functional love as a result of this personal friendship.

EPILOGUE

I trust that I have left no doubt in anyone's mind that it is love and not libido that is the principle of life, and that conflicts in the area of sexuality spring from the inability to love or be loved. In parents, the capacity to love well, that is, to love unselfishly with their feelings as well as their will, is a necessary condition for the successful development of their children into masculine men and feminine women.

The same holds true for priests and their parishioners, teachers and their pupils, physicians and nurses and their patients, persons in authority and their subjects. The words of St. Paul in his First Letter to the Corinthians apply to every one of these relationships: "*caritas aedificat*" (love builds). St. Paul was a city dweller and was familiar with urban symbols. In his Letter to the Ephesians (2:20-22) he had stated that the Christian community is "a building which rises on the foundation of the apostles and prophets, with Christ Jesus himself as the capstone" and the whole structure "takes shape as a holy temple in the Lord." Hence, love builds an edifice, a dwelling where the other can be safe and secure and can grow. This love is the generous restraining love of which I have spoken frequently and I would like to elaborate on its exact meaning.

Generous gift love. If I value my fellow human being as a good in himself, my love will go out to him. I will give him first of all the gift of myself, of wanting to be for him, to do for him, to make him happy. In addition, I will give him other things that are good for him, and since love is resourceful, these things will be numerous. But this generous gift love will always be adapted to the circumstances and needs of the one loved. For example, a mother gives her love to her infant child in a way that differs from that given to her grown-up son; a man's love for his best friend will differ from his love for his wife.

The acceptance of love. If someone offers me his love and his gifts of love, he expects me to accept his love and his gifts. By so doing, I show my love for him and do so in a most adequate way. The Flemish poet, Albert Verwey, put it succinctly: "That you allowed me to say 'I love you, I love you,' is better than all the many gifts you bestowed on me." This is well worth thinking about in our utilitarian and commercial custom of returning gift for gift, Christmas card for Christmas card, dinner for dinner.

If, however, I refuse to accept the love of the other or do so with indifference, the other may still continue to love me, but something is missing, because love should be mutual. It is also characteristic of our cold and indifferent society, as Leon Bloy has said, that its greatest sin is not to love enough, when so many are waiting for someone to respond to their love. In most cases love will ultimately die if repeatedly rejected or accepted with coldness and indifference.

Restraining love. It is evident that if I love someone generously, I will refrain from doing anything to harm the one I love; rather, I will do all in my power to do good to that person and to protect him from harm. I will also — and this is the essential element in this type of love which is least understood and developed — restrain myself in giving and receiving love when the other person is not yet capable of handling such a degree of love.

In other words, I do not force myself or my gifts on the other person nor do I demand a love of which the other person is not capable of giving. At that stage my love must take the form of simply being at hand, of quietly waiting until the other person has developed the capacity to return my love. But this waiting does not cause me to be impatient or unhappy; on the contrary, if my feelings are fully integrated into my volitional love, my willingness to wait, to hold back, to restrain myself, enables me to experience the joy of loving.

The need for this restraining love stems from the fact that love has to be free, it cannot be forced, and this is especially true of emotional love. As I have already stated, if love is to produce joy and happiness, it is not sufficient that one see the other as good and deserving of love; one must experience the feeling of love, which stimulates desire and terminates in the joy of loving. A good can be proposed to me but the love for it must come from within. Any attempt to force me to love it, or to impose on me certain ways of expressing my love, is wrong and harmful. Love must be given and accepted in freedom; constraint kills love.

The restraining love of parents and educators is especially important in the rearing of children, for it prevents them from demanding that children love grown-ups or God in a manner for which they are not yet ready. It allows them to grow up with respect and appreciation for their individuality; it patiently awaits the natural emergence of individual characteristics rather than anticipating them.

Restraining love is also necessary for young adults in their social relationships and in the period of engagement before marriage. A loving concern for the well-being of the other person will determine the proper limits of behavior. Whether two individuals are really meant for each other is not determined by experimenting with sexual activity but by their ability to experience joy in restraining themselves out of love and respect for the other.

Likewise in marriage, restraining love is needed lest one partner force himself or herself on the other by demanding, for example, the marital right when conditions are not conducive to it. It also makes it possible for husband and wife to space the number of their children without tensions and anxiety and without the use of contraceptives, which simply increase selfishness.

In the formation and guidance of candidates for the priesthood and religious life, restraining love exercised by the authorities and superiors will permit the young people to develop freely and naturally. We find an excellent example in the Mother Abbess in *The Sound of Music*. While some of the nuns criticized Maria for being different, and others smothered her with attention, the Abbess was able to let Maria be herself and to wait patiently until her love had matured enough to lead her to her goal, whether that was to be religious life or marriage.

One more area in which restraining love is needed, though of necessity it will be as yet imperfect and consist chiefly in volitional love, is the relationship among young religious and seminarians. Having heard and read so much about the need to love and be loved, they may try to force those feelings within themselves and for one another instead of waiting patiently until they have reached sufficient maturity to do this. They may take comfort in the realization that one can still develop maturity in the sorrow of not possessing what one desires, as long as one keeps the desire and hope alive and does not resort to repression.

The final question: How can one recognize mature human love, other than by the ill effects its absence causes, as in the frustration neurosis? I would propose that mature human love has the following characteristics:

First, *it is unselfish*. In true love a person recognizes the good of the other as at least equal to his own, and he will want for the other what he wants for himself. This is simply another way of stating the Golden Rule: "Love others as you love yourself." The good of the other, independent of one's subjective feelings, is what should determine one's behavior. It is the hallmark of restraining love, which is expressed in the unselfish serving of the other.

Secondly, mature love is *open to and receptive of the other*; it is disposed to *be* for the other. Then, when the other's love is accepted, that is a means of supporting and affirming the other in his or her very existence. The chief condition for this openness is to accept the other in his "otherness" and not try to remake him in my image and likeness. Too often we turn away from another because we cannot accept his or her "otherness."

Thirdly, mature love is *tender and mild when confronted with the other person's insufficiency or inadequacy*. This means that I must not measure the other in a cold and calculating fashion, but that my love enables me to empathize with him in his sufferings and needs. This will awaken in me the tenderness of compassion, of suffering with the one I love, of accepting his good intentions together with his limitations, and to do so with sympathetic understanding. Then, because of the tenderness of my love, the other will feel safe and will dare to entrust himself to me.

Finally, truly mature human love is *simple and devoid of self-conceit and pride*. This is so because the recognition of the other's good as at least equal to my own, keeps me modest and humble. In a sense, self-conceit and pride are the offspring of exaggerated self-love, which is directly contrary to the generous and mature love that is friendship love (*amor amicitiae*).

SUGGESTED READINGS

Alba House, Staten Island, NY:
   Healing the Unaffirmed (1976),
   Psychic Wholeness and Healing (1981), by A.A. Terruwe &
   C.W. Baars.
Crowell-Collier, NY:
   The Image of Love (1961), by C. Benda.
Franciscan Herald Press, Chicago, IL:
   The Crisis in the Priesthood (1972),
   A Priest for All Seasons: Masculine and Celibate (1972),
   Born Only Once (1975), by C.W. Baars;
   About Love (1974), by Josef Pieper.
Harcourt, Brace & World, Inc., NY:
   The Four Loves (1960), by C.S. Lewis.
Kenedy, NY:
   Healthy Attitudes towards Love and Sex (1964), by C.J.
   Trimbos.
Newman Press, Westminster, MD:
   Nature, Grace and Religious Development (1964), by B.
   McLaughlin.
W.W. Norton & Co., New York:
   Love and Will (1969), by Rollo May.
Paulist Press, Glen Rock, NJ:
   The Church and Sex (1959), by R.F. Trevett;
   Emotional Growth in Marriage (1968), by A.A. Terruwe.

Rockliff, London:
   Essay on Human Love (1951), by J. Guitton.
TAN Books, Rockford, IL:
   Spirituality of Love (1965), by C.V. Heris.
   Templegate, Springfield, IL:
   Marriage a Great Sacrament (1954), by J. Leclercq.